FOUNDATIONS OF MODERN PSYCHOLOGY SERIES

Richard S. Lazarus, *Editor*

RICHARD S. LAZARUS

Professor of Psychology, University of California, Berkeley; Diplomate in Clinical Psychology; author of several textbooks in personality and clinical psychology and of numerous research articles; authority on stress, his experimental work currently being supported on grant from the United States Public Health Service.

Personality
and Adjustment

PRENTICE-HALL, INC., *Englewood Cliffs, New Jersey*

PERSONALITY AND ADJUSTMENT, *Richard S. Lazarus*

PRENTICE-HALL FOUNDATIONS OF MODERN PSYCHOLOGY SERIES

Richard S. Lazarus, *Editor*

Fourth printing..... February, 1965

Designed by Harry Rinehart

C 65770

Foundations
of Modern Psychology
Series

The tremendous growth and vitality of psychology and its increasing fusion with the social and biological sciences demand a new approach to teaching at the introductory level. The basic course, geared as it usually is to a single text that tries to skim everything—that sacrifices depth for superficial breadth —is no longer adequate. Psychology has become too diverse for any one man, or a few men, to write about with complete authority. The alternative, a book that ignores many essential areas in order to present more comprehensively and effectively a particular aspect or view of psychology, is also insufficient. For in this solution, many key areas are simply not communicated to the student at all.

The Foundations of Modern Psychology is a new and different approach to the introductory course. The instructor is offered a series of short volumes, each a self-contained book on the special issues, methods, and content of a basic topic by a noted authority who is actively contributing to that particular field. And taken together, the volumes cover the full scope of psychological thought, research, and application.

The result is a series that offers the advantage of tremendous flexibility and scope. The teacher can choose the subjects he wants to emphasize and present them in the order he desires. And without necessarily sacrificing breadth, he can provide the student with a much fuller treatment of individual areas at the introductory level than is normally possible. If he does not have time to include all the volumes in his course, he can recommend the omitted ones as outside reading, thus covering the full range of psychological topics.

Psychologists are becoming increasingly aware of the importance of reaching the introductory student with high-quality, well-written, and stimulating material, material that highlights the continuing and exciting search for new knowledge. The Foundations of Modern Psychology Series is our attempt to place in the hands of instructors the best textbook tools for this purpose.

TO MY DEAR CHILDREN, DAVID AND NANCY

Preface

There are three choices an author has to make in presenting the field of personality and adjustment in the limited space of one hundred or so pages. First, he can offer a systematic viewpoint within which to encompass the field, either borrowing from one of the many theoretical treatments available, or creating a new one of his own. Second, he can attempt to summarize or review the theories and empirical findings that make up the subject matter of the field. Third, he can survey the field from the point of view of the main problems and issues, showing the ways they are resolved; in this approach he would bring in research findings only to illustrate these matters, and to serve as prototypes of the scientific efforts designed to deal with them.

I do not consider the first choice especially suitable for an introductory text. The issues are too early crystallized into particular solutions. This approach fails to offer a broad enough perspective and it deprives the student of a sense of the field as a frontier of knowledge. The second choice is impractical, partly because there is simply too much to be wisely condensed into a short treatment, and partly because the theories and findings are apt to become so much nonsense material which the student will memorize and soon forget without having gained an awareness of the fundamental questions themselves.

I have adopted the third solution for this book in the conviction that the greatest sense of order and the broadest perspective can be achieved by discussing the main issues personality theorists have attempted to resolve, the issues which have been the subject of empirical research. What emerges, then, is an introduction to a rich world of ideas for the person who wishes to know how and why as well as what. I hope that the reader, armed with an awareness of the questions and problems provided here, will make further and more meaningful explorations into man's knowledge and speculations about personality and adjustment.

Richard S. Lazarus

Contents

Contents

Introduction

At no time in the history of mankind has concern been so widespread about the problems of personal adjustment, nor interest so intense in human personality, as it is today, particularly in the United States and the rest of the western world. On all sides we are besieged by statistics about mental health and personality disorder. Inspirational books and articles abound that exhort us to achieve, each in some particular way, psychological tranquillity and interpersonal effectiveness. We also hear widespread expressions of anxiety about the subtle but powerful social pressures toward conformity, which, to the personality psychologist, is one of the solutions people adopt in their struggle to master the stresses of social living.

Perhaps one major reason for the growth of interest in adjustment and personality is the change in man's status in his physical environment. In the most technically advanced societies he has conquered the earth on which he lives, by subduing other beasts, reducing the inroads of disease-producing microörganisms, and growing magnificent crops more and more efficiently wrested from the land. He can travel with knowledge and confidence under and on the sea, and he can transport himself through the air with safety and unbelievable speed. With his control of electricity and various forms of radiation, he can propel his sounds and images anywhere he wishes and so communicate almost instantaneously with people anywhere in the world. Thus, with his mind, man has come to control his physical environment.

Yet in spite of his enormous power of adaptation, man recognizes that he remains today, as in centuries past, a victim of himself. He faces annihilation at the hands of his own kind through the very technical advances that help free him from other elemental struggles. So he fears other men. And to master this fear he must understand mankind and what organizes its behavior. So with his previously acquired logical understanding of nature, and having rejected demons and magic as explanations for human problems, he turns to an examination of himself as a social and biological creature. He is aware of powerful emotional struggles within him that dominate his behavior and threaten his sense of well-being, and to deal with these struggles effectively he must understand them, too. Thus, for practical reasons as well as because of intellectual curiosity, he strives to enable the understanding of psychological man to catch up with the understanding of the physical world.

The psychologist interested in adjustment and personality focuses distinctively on the person. He views the person as a whole, as an organized system, and although he considers the person to be made up of individual structures and functions, he is aware that the particular elements have no true separate identity. The unifying concepts of adjustment and personality include the various subordinate processes of motivation, emotion, and cognition, but these are regarded as being organized into a larger system, the personality, which has transactions with, or adjusts to, the physical and social world. It is by means of these functions that the person accomplishes the tasks of adjustment, but these functions are not the person.

The fields of personality and adjustment are closely related because the processes of adjustment depend on the stable structures of personality, and personality has to do with the consistent ways in which the person adjusts to the environment. For purposes of exposition, however, we shall treat these concepts separately, recognizing that they represent slightly different aspects of the total person as seen in the world in which he lives. We begin with the concept of adjustment and the special problem of conflict.

Conflict
and Adjustment

According to the dictionary the verb "to adjust" means to fit, to make correspondent, to adapt, or to accommodate. Thus, when we adjust something we change it in some way to make it appropriate to certain requirements—for example, extending a ladder so it is the right height to reach a second-story window. As used in psychology, the term means that we must accommodate ourselves in order to fit certain demands of our environment. Therefore, the study of adjustment has to do with how we make such accommodations and how successfully they fit us to the demands that are made on us. *Adjustment consists of the processes by means of which we manage these demands.*

3

1

What are these demands to which a person must adjust and what is their source? Some originate in sources outside him, whereas others have their origin in tissue activity within.

External Demands

The most important external demands that challenge a man's adjustive capacities arise from his social environment, from living in society interdependently with other persons. These demands begin when, as an infant, a person depends for comfort and security on the benevolence and wisdom of his parents, who must be willing and able to provide essential care. Then, later, the social institutions of the culture into which he is born demand conformity to certain social values and culturally developed patterns of behavior. Throughout life these various demands are expressed as expectations that others have of him. For example, a man is expected to marry and have a family, work at an occupation and fit into a status hierarchy, and live in certain ways that are appropriate to his place in the society. Husbands expect certain behavior from their wives, and wives of their husbands; employers similarly expect prescribed behavior patterns from their employees, and employees anticipate complementary behavior in return. And so it goes, implicitly or explicitly, with parents and children, friends or business associates, and in all manner of complex relationships that constitute the structure of the society in which we live.

These expectations are usually enforced by the threat of physical punishment or of psychological penalties such as ostracism and disapproval. They operate as powerful pressures on an individual to which he must accommodate if he is to have comfortable and effective intercourse with his social environment.

Internal Demands

The internal demands that originate in tissue activity are often called physiological needs. Man is born with a number of such needs, whose satisfaction is required to preserve his life and comfort. Although these needs are inborn, people must learn what satisfies each particular need in order to do something about it. Most of these physiological needs such as temperature regulation, sleep, hunger and thirst can be gratified through intentional adjustive behavior, for example, wearing appropriate clothing, going to bed, eating and drinking. Psychologists often call physiological needs primary because they automatically arise from our inherited structure. But recently many psychologists have been expressing dissatisfaction with the traditional list of primary needs, for they have increasingly recognized the primary nature of such activities as exploration, manipulation, and mastery. And they have proposed adding those activities to the traditional list of inherited needs. In any event, needs of all kinds energize and direct both human and animal behavior.

Sometimes, demands that were originally external become internal through the process of *socialization*. That is, when a child is young his parents demand from him certain forms of behavior and the acceptance of certain social values, and they enforce their regulations by reward and punishment, approval and disapproval. Somehow a child comes to accept many of these values of society as they are communicated by the parents and he internalizes them so that they become an integral part of his personality. Precisely how he does so is a fascinating, as yet unresolved, theoretical issue. But in any event, our sense of right and wrong and our need for achievement or esteem do not arise directly from our physiological construction; rather, we learn them from experience in the society we live in. All men share, in the main, the same physiological needs, but it is evident that people who grow up in different societies often have radically different sets of values and patterns of social motivation.

Although social values and motives are learned, they continue to operate throughout life as powerful energizing and directing forces in behavior. They may even become potent enough to overcome physiological survival needs. Political and religious martyrs, for example, have been willing to suffer great pain and even die for principles in which they believed intensely. It is evident, then, that because of the process of socialization, or internalization of external demands, internal needs ultimately include not only the primary physiological urges native to the human animal but also learned, social motivations peculiar to each particular society. And we must adjust to both kinds of internal demand.

Since great suffering can attend a person's failure to meet many of the external and internal demands to which he is exposed, adjustment is a matter of behaving in such a way that he can lessen this suffering by reducing the number and intensity of demands. But he may face serious obstacles to the success of this effort. Sometimes the means to gratify needs are not available. Then, too, level of intelligence, specific skills, and good and bad fortune can contribute to the success or failure of need-reduction. And most importantly, an inevitable and powerful source of need-thwarting springs up when the demands that require adjustive behavior are in conflict.

CONFLICT BETWEEN DEMANDS

Conflict occurs when two demands that are being made on a person are incompatible—that is, when the behavior compelled by one makes it impossible for him to do what is called for by another. He is thus pulled between two opposing psychological forces, and he cannot satisfy the one without failing to gratify the other.

Suppose, for example, that a person sustains the wish to be strong and self-sufficient, masterful and decisive, and that he normally conceives of himself in this way. Yet suppose also that he has equally strong security needs, deeply longing to be cared for by someone just as he had been sheltered and protected in childhood by his mother. Regardless of the origins of this state of affairs, a motivational conflict exists that is likely to have serious ramifications in his behavior and emotional life. For each step he takes in the direction of courageously and independently facing the world and its problems fills him with dread because such independent activity is incompatible with his wish to be protected and reassured. And conversely, every act or feeling oriented toward support and protection by mothering persons thwarts his desire to be independent and so threatens the picture of himself that reflects this desire. Thus, one set of needs cannot be fulfilled without thwarting the other. People actually do learn many different ways of dealing with such a conflict, but here, clearly, the presence of conflict renders the gratification of both needs enormously complicated if not impossible.

Let us consider for a moment what types of conflict are possible and which are most important. We can analyze conflict in two ways: We can either look to the origins of the conflict—that is, whether the demands that are incompatible are mainly internal or external—or we can identify a person's reactions to demands—that is, whether his responses are characterized by approach (a positive orientation to a demand) or avoidance (a negative orientation).

Conflict Classified by Source

There are three principal patterns of conflict. First, friction may develop *between internal and external demands*. This is the predominant source of conflict early in life when a person has not yet internalized very many values of his society. Trouble arises when an individual wants or needs something that runs counter to pressures or demands from without—for example, the organized patterns of roles and behaviors he is expected to follow as a member of a particular culture. Thus, following a frustrating experience, a young child may become angry and attack the thing or person he thinks is at the root of the trouble. But he soon probably discovers two things: The person he assaults in anger, be it another child or an adult, may retaliate and leave him doubly hurt; and adults may enjoin him from fighting or breaking objects, reinforcing these admonitions by threats of punishment or by anxiety-producing disapproval.

The process of accepting the discipline of the social world early in life may start up an intense struggle and may help to set the stage for his attitudes toward, and ways of dealing with, frustration for many years to come. But whatever the particular need involved, in this type of conflict a need directly confronts external demands that are incompatible with it or that require postponing its gratification or satisfying it only through socially acceptable forms.

To illustrate this latter instance, although adults in modern Western society are constrained from expressing physical aggression toward others, and often even from direct verbal assault (which is not considered quite so bad), they are permitted a number of socially acceptable outlets for discharging anger. These socially acceptable forms for handling aggressive impulses represent still another attempt to resolve conflict between external and internal demands. Consider a person who has a strong trait of aggressiveness. He usually cannot, without reproach or retaliation from the people around him, express these impulses readily. Expressing them might even lead to his being jailed. But he can attend a boxing match and discharge his anger vicariously toward one of the professional fighters who is being beaten up, or angrily boo a dull fight (which is usually characterized by a limited measure of physical punishment). Or still better, he may, if he is able, fight professionally himself; at least he can participate in amateur boxing or in other physical-contact sports, such as wrestling, basketball, hockey, or football. Even these team sports require body blocking and an aggressive spirit of competition.

On the intellectual side, too, release is possible: A chronically angry person can become a professional critic or a "sick" comic; with complete propriety he can speak out against all sorts of evils in society and attack political candidates and parties; and he can express his anger in many similar ways that do not normally lead to retaliation, criticism, or punishment by society. In expressing anger or any other set of internal needs in a socially acceptable fashion, we often succeed in reducing conflict by transforming the internal needs, perhaps by delaying their expression, and by coming to terms with external demands that are in conflict with the original form of the internal need. But we shall have more to say later about the resolution of conflict when we discuss the process of adjustment.

Just as conflict is possible between internal and external demands, so *two external demands may be in conflict.* The psychoanalyst Karen Horney wrote extensively about this subject, emphasizing the importance of cultural conflicts. She noted many examples of values within a culture or between subcultures of a society that are inconsistent and incompatible. For instance, from childhood we are told formally (in school, church, and home) to love our neighbor and to regard him with kindness and humility. At the same time, in direct conflict with this verbally expressed value, we are also encouraged to be aggressive and individualistic and to compete with others. Thus, the philosophy of "turning the other cheek" is in sharp conflict with the actual value system that is revealed a large part of the time in the behavior of those who set constant examples to the developing child. So, as he matures, a child absorbs two incompatible values, and that incompatibility contributes to the formation of neurotic conflict. In most societies, maturing requires some resolution of the many conflicting external demands to which an individual is inevitably exposed.

The third major type of conflict occurs *between two internal demands*— that is to say, two needs or values we carry around because of physiological characteristics or the internalization of cultural patterns. A simple example might make this clear. As you sit and read these pages you may be experiencing fatigue and you may find your eyes gradually tending to close. But the requirement that you absorb the material (although it may originate in an external source—that is, the teacher, parental expectations, and so forth— the need to achieve or cultivate knowledge has probably become internalized) makes you struggle against the tendency to doze. So a conflict exists between two needs, both now internal. Such conflict may occur even without a person's awareness and when this happens we say that one or both of the needs involved is unconscious.

In the case of your immediate struggle between sleepiness and the need to absorb the subject matter of this volume, the conflict is relatively minor (unless you are facing a crucial examination in the morning). And many conflicts are of just such a nature, being too weak to have serious consequences for one's adjustment. In other instances, however, such internal conflict may occur between two extremely powerful yet incompatible needs; then the task of making a satisfactory adjustment is far more difficult. Under such circumstances signs of stress are likely to emerge.

It might be noted in passing that adequacy or inadequacy of adjustment may be a matter less of the amount of conflict to which a person is exposed than of the extent to which he has learned techniques of mastery that permit satisfactory solutions to conflict. The crucial aspect of the problem is the availability of some response that meets the situation successfully. This is an important and interesting issue that psychologists need to solve before they can fully understand why some people develop in a healthy way and others do not. Still, there is nothing unusual about conflict. In a sense it is banal, but it is important to understand what conflict is, because failure to deal with it successfully is tantamount to mental illness and great suffering.

Lewin's Classification of Conflict

The second way to classify types of conflict we mentioned above was devised by Kurt Lewin, an illustrious theoretician in the field of personality and social processes. He based his classification on the human tendency to approach or avoid stimuli that the person regards as beneficial or harmful. For Lewin, approach or avoidance was not necessarily a physical act of locomotion but could be a purely mental event. Lewin distinguished three basic types of conflict: approach-approach, avoidance-avoidance, and approach-avoidance.

In *approach-approach conflict* a person is simultaneously drawn to two positive goals that are equally attractive, so he has difficulty deciding on which to go toward. For example, a child may have trouble in choosing between watching a favorite program on television and playing baseball with his friends up the street. In *avoidance-avoidance conflict* two negative goals are involved, neither of which is desirable. A student, for example, may be impelled to choose between spending many hours studying for an examination or risking the danger of failure, though he regards neither the studying nor the failure as pleasant. Finally, in *approach-avoidance conflict,* which appears to be the most difficult to resolve, a person is attracted to a goal by which he is also repelled. For instance, a child may seek to watch a horror movie while remaining fearful about the terror and distress it may cause him. He is both favorably and unfavorably disposed to the experience at the same time. Similarly, to a shy individual the prospect of a date may appear as both a desirable event and a source of anxiety because he is not sure whether he will know how to act. Clearly, analyzing conflict in terms of approach and avoidance offers a new perspective by emphasizing a person's reaction tendencies toward conflicting goals rather than the internal or external origins of the conflict.

The conflicts that characterize us are often inevitable consequences of our biological make-up and the nature of the society in which we live. Yet many conflicts do not necessarily exist objectively but result from the way we perceive situations. For example, conflict is not necessarily inescapable between the common desire in modern Western culture to be successful and the equally frequent wish to be accepted, approved, or liked by others. But a person may regard these desires as incompatible. Because of the way he has learned to perceive the world about him, he may fear that, if he competes successfully against others and thus achieves success, others will react punitively to this success. He assumes that they too aim for success and will resent his attainment, and since he also wishes to be accepted and liked he may find it difficult or impossible to enter into competition. Caught between two forces he thinks are incompatible, he may behave so that he appears irrational to others. Thus, on the verge of success he may do something that produces sudden failure. Because of the conflict he creates out of his own interpretation of the situation, he is impotent to reach either of his goals.

Although we have been discussing conflict between internal and external demands, we have not yet systematically addressed ourselves to the problem of the sources of this conflict—that is, the actual nature of the fundamental internal and external demands to which we must adjust. The solution to this problem turns out to depend to a large extent on personality theory, which we shall consider more fully in Chapters 4 and 5. There we shall attempt to delineate theoretical differences about basic human needs. And because different theories of personality offer different answers, the question is complex and must be deferred for a while.

THE RESOLUTION OF CONFLICT

Implicit in our discussion so far is the idea that a person's comfort, happiness, and effectiveness depend on his success in resolving conflicts. As we have described conflict up to now it might seem at first glance that a person in conflict has no more than a tricky intellectual problem to solve. And to some degree competence in reducing environmental demands and gratifying basic needs does depend on knowledge, skill, and understanding of the fundamentals of social living. But conflict does produce a very special danger, especially when two strong internal needs are at issue. It is that one or both of the needs, however important, must remain unsatisfied, and this is a continuing source of anxiety and distress.

We can probably make this point clearer by elaborating our earlier example of conflict between the wish to be independent and autonomous and the need for security and dependence. This is a crisis that is faced most acutely by an adolescent who is separating himself from home. Indeed, many influential personality theorists assign this kind of struggle fundamental importance in the development of personality. As we said above, achieving one goal cannot be accomplished without thwarting the other. On the surface, at least, both needs seem utterly incompatible. Yet there are countless small battlegrounds in life on which this struggle is fought, and in each struggle a person must make strategic decisions. For example, he may have to decide any of the following: whether to remain in his present job, where he is secure and knows what to expect, or to risk taking another, where the outcome is less certain but the prospects of advancement are greater; whether to leave home and get married or to remain in the haven of his parental nest; whether to speak out in disagreement with his peers, friends, and associates or to avoid open hostility or disapproval by agreeing with them or remaining silent;

whether to ask a superior for help or for reassurance that he is doing the job correctly at each step of the way or to find and apply his own solutions, presenting them in the face of possible criticism or ridicule. In countless other instances of this basic conflict, security and support are pitted against individuality and self-direction. Clearly, it takes more than intelligence and knowledge to master such a problem.

ADJUSTMENT BY ACCOMMODATION OR ASSIMILATION

Two fundamental solutions—accommodation and assimilation—seem possible when conflict arises. In *accommodation*, a person can subordinate one of the conflicting pressures and choose to express and gratify the other. Thus, when the conflict is between a personally centered urge and a socially oriented value a person may alter himself and reject the personal goal in favor of the social direction, for he may not feel that the expression of individuality is worth either the suffering produced by the criticism and rejection of others or the self-censure that may be generated. In short, he subordinates and accommodates himself to the social environment. Although such tendencies to conformity have come to have unpleasant overtones in the literature of our times, they are also an essential part of growing up, since some degree of acceptance of social norms is necessary for society to exist and, to some extent, for a person to lead a reasonably effective life. The desirability or undesirability of accommodative solutions to conflicts is by no means simple to determine and must be evaluated against the degree to which a person submerges essential parts of himself in order to gain social acceptance. An especially interesting problem arises when adults accommodate without being aware that inner needs or values are being submerged.

In a classic experiment in social psychology, the distinguished research psychologist Solomon Asch produced an important experimental analogue of this accommodative, or conformist, solution to conflict between individual desire and social pressure. He set up several groups, all of whose members except the critical subject had been instructed in advance about how to behave in the experimental situation. Each person in each group of eight was required to make a series of perceptual judgments and, one by one, to express them in public. The task was to match the length of a standard line to that of three comparison lines, one that was about the same length as, and two that deviated noticeably from, the standard. The task was actually simple. When there was no social pressure and judgments were given privately, the critical subjects made no errors. When the judgments were expressed publicly, however, each of the informed subjects gave as his best judgment the same wrong answer, which was at variance with the critical subject's judgment. Under these conditions the answer given by the key subject often conformed to that of the group. That even in so unambiguous a task, subjects' judgments were made to conform to the group about 30 per cent of the time indicates the power of social pressure.

Subsequent interviews with participants, wherein the experimenter confronted them with their answers, also helped reveal the processes involved in conformist behavior. Some subjects said they had changed their judgment because they thought that they had misunderstood the situation. Others admitted they could not accept the distress of being the only one responding differently. A small number seemed to have been unaware that they had even conformed to the group pressure and appeared surprised when their actual answers to each perceptual problem were pointed out. These last cases appear to illustrate an unconscious accommodative solution to conflict whereby a person presumably eschews accurate perception of reality without being aware of doing so. (As we shall discover later, such unconscious adjustive efforts are ego-defense mechanisms whereby an individual deceives himself about actual circumstances or about impulses he cannot accept in himself.) In this way the individual partly solves the dilemma of conflict, because he no longer has to acknowledge its existence. For he gives up or denies internal needs that are at variance with external (or internalized) social demands (although, as we shall see later, this kind of solution may have pathological consequences).

Assimilation, the other solution to conflict, requires mastering, or eliminating, or rejecting, the social demand rather than giving up the personal need. In this process a person assimilates the world to his own requirements, using people and social situations about him most advantageously for attaining his own ends. The term "interpersonal competence" has been used by psychologists and sociologists to stand for social skills that permit a person to control to a high degree his social affairs so that he may successfully develop along self-chosen lines.

The kinds of solution to conflict we have been discussing usually evolve out of a strenuous struggle. Indeed, in the experiment by Asch which was cited above, many subjects made their judgments independently, in spite of the pressure of the group. Some of them appeared to do so out of a sense of confidence in their perception and experience. Others were independent, but withdrawn—sensitive to the group, experiencing keenly the conflict, but aware of the necessity of remaining individuals. Still others made the independent judgment with tension and doubt, yet felt it necessary to deal as adequately as possible with the task itself. All these instances represent assimilative solutions to conflict, each group gratifying somewhat different internal needs at the expense of the external demands toward conformity.

One of the obstacles standing in the way of creative and effective conflict-resolution is the frequent failure of a person to recognize the basic forces that underlie his personal conflicts. If he is unaware of these forces, then the conflicts themselves will be inaccessible to intentional solution.

CONFLICT, STRESS, AND ADJUSTMENT

One of the chief reasons why people resort to inadequate solutions of conflict is that states of stress generally attend strong conflict and the thwarting of powerful motives. Stress complicates the solution of conflicts in several ways. In the first place, there is evidence that the affective aspects of stress (for example, anxiety and depression) interfere with thinking and problem-solving and may thus reduce a person's effectiveness in mastering a situation. Anxiety, for example, has been shown to interfere under certain conditions with attention-span and with the learning of complex material. Exposing people to stressful situations has also been known to narrow their perceptual field, making them less aware of features of their environment and less able to utilize relevant information in the solution of their problems. Although states of stress do not always have such destructive consequences (they even appear sometimes to mobilize individuals toward more effective performance), there is little doubt that under many circumstances they also impede the resolution of conflict and the solution of life problems.

The second way stress complicates the solution to conflict is by being extremely painful. Consequently, it may motivate a person to find means to reduce or eliminate it regardless of any consequences in maladjustment. The defense mechanism is such a means. For example, by denying the existence of conflict or the demands that generate it, an individual need not concern himself consciously with the problem. If he can sell himself on the idea that he is not hostile toward someone, doesn't fear something, or doesn't have unacceptable sexual urges, he can eliminate the feeling of disturbance that comes from apprehending the dilemma of conflict. The situation is reinterpreted and psychic danger seems to exist no longer because of self-deception.

Stress produced by conflict may, therefore, motivate defensive activity designed to reduce or eliminate it at the expense of an objective, or realistic, appraisal of the actual situation. Since as a result of such defenses an individual is not aware of the conflict, he cannot possibly do anything constructive about it. And, according to the theory of defense mechanism, these tricks of self-deception do not succeed in actually eliminating the impulses they were designed to remove, only the awareness of them. Thus, they confuse the person about reality, leading him therefore to inappropriate decisions based on an incorrect appraisal of circumstances. So, while hatred toward a sibling, parent, or spouse is defensively denied, the hostile impulses may remain, even though unconsciously, and continue to disrupt the person's relationships with others. But we shall say more about defense-mechanisms shortly.

Adequacy of Adjustment and the Problem of Mental Health

One of the most difficult and challenging problems in the psychology of adjustment is the matter of evaluating the adequacy of adjustment. There are many practical reasons why we might wish to make such evaluations. In clinical work, for example, they would be useful in determining who needs psychotherapy. In industry, too, they would be valuable to personnel departments, which prefer for reasons of effectiveness to hire well-adjusted candidates to fill jobs ranging from the most routine to the highest level. The military services need to screen out men who are emotionally disturbed at the time of induction or who are

2

likely to become so under the stresses of military life and combat. And teachers are interested in aiding young people who are wasting educational opportunities because of inadequacies of adjustment. In all these cases, standards for determining adequacy of adjustment would be very useful.

As we become more sophisticated in understanding the process of adjustment, however, we become more aware of the difficulties of agreeing upon criteria of maladjustment. The many different criteria now being used in professional practice are often contradictory and are difficult to apply, so they raise serious questions about what mental health is. The crux of the problem, of course, is how to determine our criteria scientifically, for we cannot say what is good and bad in adjustment without making value judgments. And value judgments are based on opinions of what is desirable and undesirable in people and in society. We want to come back to this point, but first we shall discuss the principal current criteria of maladjustment. The emphasis is on maladjustment because specialists have been much more explicit about symptoms of adjustive failure than about the signs of successful adjustment, or mental health.

CRITERIA OF MALADJUSTMENT

The presence of a characteristic high degree of *psychological discomfort* in an individual over a long time is one obvious criterion, obvious because a person who is chronically anxious or depressed is poignantly aware that his life is not all that it might be. Indeed, the psychological pain and misery he suffers often lead him to seek professional help. Of course, the fact of being in treatment is often misleading as a sign of poor adjustment, since many persons who are far more uncomfortable pychologically than the individual in therapy may refuse to seek assistance or be unable to do so for financial or other reasons. Although psychological discomfort is usually taken as a sign of inadequate adjustment, we shall see later that the converse—psychological comfort—is not necessarily a sign of successful adjustment.

Cognitive inefficiency is another criterion of maladjustment. The inability of the person to think clearly without distortion of reality or to exercise social and occupational skills as he once did may signify a state of stress and its consequent disturbance of adjustment. Many mentally ill patients have long —sometimes lifelong—histories of general intellectual and social inadequacy, including failure in school, failure to take responsibilities commensurate with age, and inability to get and hold jobs for any substantial length of time. It also happens that, after many years of high-level functioning a person may exhibit a sudden (in a matter of weeks or months) deterioration of judgment, of his ability to solve problems and to size up social realities correctly. Commonly, such an individual, unaware of how far his performance has declined, is at a loss to explain the attitudes and behavior of others toward him. Sometimes, though, the loss of normal adequacy may be what drives him to therapy. Since a decline in intellectual and social effectiveness is likely to be an aspect of disturbed adjustment, it becomes also a major criterion of adjustive failure.

In recent years we have become aware that difficulties in the process of adjustment may be reflected in *disturbances of body functioning* and in damage to body tissues—a third criterion of adjustive inadequacy. Typical psychosomatic symptoms are impairment of appetite, high blood pressure, migraine headache, persistent diarrhea, gastrointestinal pains, and ulcers of the stomach, duodenum, and large intestines which may ultimately rupture, bleed, and even cause death. A person who is afflicted may be quite unaware of the psychological origin of these symptoms. But if they have no detectable physical cause and if they respond favorably to improvement in the circumstances of his life or to psychotherapy, we can reasonably ascribe to them a psychological basis. A particularly fascinating research problem is the quest for the precise psychodynamics and physiological mechanisms of these disturbances.

A fourth major criterion of adjustive failure is *deviation in behavior* from social norms. Extreme deviation, of course, can lead to a person's hospitalization, because such behavior often seriously violates social propriety or leads others to fear for their own or the disturbed person's safety.

The criterion of behavior deviation is largely based on the social mores of the people with whom the maladjusted person comes in contact. If a person who is having emotional difficulties develops symptoms that happen to be socially acceptable or desirable, or manages to exhibit behavior that is in close conformity to the social norms, he will rarely be considered maladjusted. He may suffer with ulcers, for example; but in many groups this affliction is just a sign of being a "member of the club" because such a symptom of chronic stress is shared by many of his associates. But if he deviates in behavior from important social norms, the treatment accorded to him is likely to be quite different. Thus, if he has a penchant for telling risqué stories in the wrong company or for adopting extreme political positions or for expressing outlandish social attitudes, he is likely to be viewed as maladjusted and as such will be shunned or punished. If the deviation is sufficiently extreme he may be hospitalized with the rationalization that he needs help. This could be quite true in many cases, but a major reason for institutionalization is often to retire an individual to some safe, locked place away from people he might offend or harm. "Crazy people" who are harmless and who manage to care for themselves are not usually hospitalized. Chiefly, then, any behavior deviations that are difficult to understand and seem threatening in some way become the basis for the designation of maladjustment and for taking active steps to "protect the community."

Difficulties in Applying the Criteria

We dwell on this point because the criterion of deviation from social norms illustrates, better than any other, some of the difficult problems of applying the criteria of adjustive adequacy. In the first place, there is the problem of *cultural relativism*. For the social norms against which adjustment is evaluated are never absolute. They vary from culture to culture and even within a culture from one group to another. Thus, social psychologists have shown that, at least some years ago, among American middle-class families physical aggression toward another child was considered bad and children were taught to inhibit it, while among lower-class families, being tough and ready to display it in assault on others was more often a basis for earning respect. And as anthropologist Margaret Mead has pointed out, Samoan boys and girls before marriage are expected to engage in exploratory sex play, whereas in our own culture we have rather strict taboos against this behavior, with the value (at least as expressed in public) that sexual activity outside of marriage is sinful. Of course, it is well known from the studies of sexual behavior in men and women in the United States made by Kinsey and his associates that this taboo is quite commonly ignored. For example, even though prostitution is illegal, Kinsey estimated on the basis of data from his sample that perhaps as many as two-thirds of adult males in the United States ultimately have some experience with prostitutes, although the incidence clearly varies greatly with educational level, being highest in the least educated groups. A high incidence was also found for other forms of extramarital and premarital sex relations. Thus, different cultures often have very different norms for behavior, so that what represents deviation in one society may be "normal" in another. Certain standards of conduct, however, which are merely superficial or simply given verbal expression, are less likely than others to be religiously followed by the population, or at least by large segments of it.

What is more, within the same society what is normal in one era may be pathological in another. For example, the ordinary dress and behavior of the modern woman would have seemed to approach the psychotic less than a hundred years ago. Even more recently, in fact, the efforts of suffragettes to establish the right of women to vote had the same taint, and it often surprises young people today to learn that women obtained this right so short a time ago as 1920. Because of this problem of cultural relativism, the application of the criterion of deviation from the social norm is largely arbitrary. Clearly, what is "normal" in behavior is difficult to evaluate scientifically since it depends so much on the culture involved.

The problem of *standards* for evaluating adjustment further complicates the task of applying our criteria. There are two general kinds of standards. One is *inter-individual*, whereby we consider one person's deviation from the standard of what others are like. But what shall this standard be? Whom will we use to establish our norms? If we could actually determine a statistical average for our country, or the world, can we claim that the "average" man is really a good standard against which to make comparisons? What degree of deviation from the norm is abnormal or pathological? How much anxiety is bad? There is no scientific way of answering these questions; we can only make arbitrary decisions. Inter-individual comparisons can be at best rough guidelines without any precise force or meaning.

The other type of standard is *intra-individual*. In this type, we obtain our norm from an estimate of a person's usual, or normal, behavior or from an estimate of the ideal level of efficiency, comfort, or bodily health he is capable of attaining. Thus, if a person who usually suffers moderately from anxiety enters a period during which his anxiety level becomes inordinately high, we may take this deviation from his own individual standard as an indication of disturbance. Similarly, if we assess his efficiency or the adequacy of his inter-personal relations at a certain typical level, then we can regard periods of decline in these characteristics as times of adjustive inadequacy. And, in fact, we often find signs of such disturbance for extended periods before psychological crises or "breakdowns." One attraction of intra-individual standards is that they are useful in overcoming a disadvantage of the inter-individual type: ignoring the resources a person is normally capable of bringing to bear on his problems.

The dilemma of choosing values in applying the criteria of adjustive adequacy is further illustrated by the frequent disagreements about what conclusions should be drawn from each of the four criteria. Some disorders—for example, conversion hysteria—are associated with high degrees of psychological comfort. This is illustrated in the case of a student who appeared at the psychological clinic of his college complaining that he could not swallow solid food. A medical inquiry revealed that he had been losing weight at a rapid rate, and an examination showed no physical defect that would account for the difficulty. It was guessed that the disorder was functional and had its origin in psychological causes. The clinical psychologist attempted to learn the source of the problem and systematically explored the student's family and school adjustments. To each inquiry the student reported nothing but the most wholesome and happy relationships with everyone. Denial of any interpersonal conflict appeared to be a characteristic pattern. As he stated in the interview, "I don't have any psychological problems. Everything is fine. It is just that I can't swallow."

The symptom, sometimes referred to as "globus hystericus," clearly indicated a neurotic disorder, known as "conversion hysteria," that is often associated with an absence of awareness of psychological stress even though such stress surely exists. Although the sufferer may express distress about the symptom itself, he will commonly deny feeling anxiety based on neurotic conflict. This absence of conflict-based anxiety has been called by clinical workers "la belle indifférence"—the beautiful lack of concern. In such a case as this, the criterion of psychological discomfort would not support a diagnosis of maladjustment, while the criterion dealing with disturbances of body functioning would indicate a very different conclusion.

Can we reasonably give certain criteria more importance than others in determining adequacy of adjustment? Is somebody who is psychologically comfortable but afflicted with a psychosomatic symptom better adjusted than someone who suffers marked anxiety or depression but shows few signs of physical disturbance or wear and tear? The answer, as we have indicated above, is a matter of opinion and arbitrary choice. It depends on which symptoms we prefer. Of course, a maladjusted person's friends might like him better if the evidences of his disturbance are internal states rather than behavioral deviation from the social norms to which they adhere. But clearly, the choice is not in the realm of science but of personal and social values.

In all the discussion above we have been touching on the problem of mental health, and in particular the problem of developing an approach to mental health that is not dominated by the negative idea of the absence of symptoms of psychopathology; this is a question that has been of increasing concern to psychologists of personality. Let us turn now to this movement to redefine mental health, a movement that is a natural outgrowth of attempts to evaluate the adequacy of adjustment.

Two conceptions of healthy personality have dominated psychological thought in recent years. The older is the *contented-cow* approach, which gauges good adjustment chiefly by the absence of signs of stress. In this view, people should accommodate successfully to their surroundings, physical and social, and should accept without stress the roles, value systems, and behavior patterns imposed upon them by the culture in which they live. A healthy person is comfortable, fulfills as efficiently as he is able the social tasks set forth by society (for example, self-employment, savings, rearing a family, and so on), is free of the physical symptoms of stress, and deviates scarcely at all from social norms. The essence of good adjustment is benignness. Anxiety is bad, symptoms of stress are bad, nonconformity to social norms is bad, and, of course, working and producing and even playing inefficiently are also bad.

Of late, however, psychologists (as well as social and political philosophers of our times) have been increasingly dissatisfied with the contented-cow approach to mental health. First, since the implied definition of mental health is negative, when a psychologist attempts to define what mental health is, rather than what it isn't, the traditional view fails to help him. Second, the ideal of conformity, comfort, and absence of stress is open to challenge as a value system, for it neglects or subordinates assimilative processes of adjustment and it misses the point that stress may be a normal part of life.

Can we not, in the Faustian tradition of Goethe, affirm that striving, even unsuccessfully, is meritorious? Can we not view anxiety as a positive and potent force that energizes and directs the great achievements of mankind? It is just this sort of thinking that has led psychologists to develop a second major conception of mental health, a view that stresses, in contrast with making accommodations to the environment by altering or giving up fundamental personal qualities, mastery of the environment, or *competence*.

Psychologists have given a variety of expressions to this emphasis on competence. One of the earliest proponents of this notion of good adjustment, Otto Rank, emphasized the individual's paradoxical creative struggle to become separated, or individuated, from the rest of mankind and yet simultaneously to achieve union with it. Recent versions of this viewpoint may be found among personality theorists such as Abraham Maslow and Carl Rogers who view successful adjustment as the achievement of self-actualization—that is, the successful expression of the highest potentialities of which a person is capable. Such theorists regard the individual not as a passive accommodator to social forces that press upon him, but as an active seeker after mastery over these social forces and the expression of his highest intellectual and esthetic potentialities. In their view, mental health, or good adjustment, is a matter of positive striving and continual growth.

One recent, well-known expression of the positive-striving point of view may be found in the writings of Marie Jahoda, who identifies as criteria of mental health such qualities as self-awareness, self-acceptance, growth, development, self-actualization, integration (or a unifying outlook and balance of psychological forces), autonomy, perception of reality free from need-distortion, and mastery of the environment. She emphasizes the individual's ability to control interpersonal relations and to succeed in self-development in individually chosen directions. And, in her view, since competence enables a person to acquire detachment and to develop his own values, a competent person is better adjusted than an incompetent one.

Clearly, these writers who emphasize positive striving and competence are expressing a point of view that is a far cry from the contented-cow conception of adjustment. Clearly, too, the differences between these two main positions stem from different value systems and philosophies, the former venerating man's adaptability, his capacity to modify himself in keeping with the demands of the world about him, the latter admiring most the person who transcends and masters his environment and who accommodates only to permit his continued development and self-expression.

RESEARCH IN MENTAL HEALTH

Since it is clear that value judgments enter into any determination of adequacy of adjustment—and indeed cannot be eliminated entirely—how is it possible to undertake scientific research on adjustment? Recognizing this problem, social psychologist M. Brewster Smith has pointed out that, although science cannot choose among values, it can objectively examine the actual consequences of various facts of our social existence, once we have accepted some particular value. Smith writes:

To the extent that there is already consensus on human values, empirical evidence, when there is some, can tell us how to maximize the values we have selected. Research can also provide the occasion for revising the existing consensus or for approaching consensus when none presently exists. Indirectly, and always in conjunction with personal choice, it furnishes grounds for re-evaluation. (From Smith, M.B., Research strategies toward a conception of positive mental health. *Amer. Psychol.*, 1959, 14, pp. 674–675.)

The point is, if we recognize that our conceptions of mental health are grounded in our personal and cultural values, we can still, by accepting or assuming these values, explore how well they are being met and what other possible personal and social consequences they may have. For example, if we were to accept the value of conformity as commendable, we could examine the degree to which people conform, in what respects, and under what conditions. Furthermore, we could determine what other consequences conformity might have—say, comfort, physical symptoms, or cognitive efficiency. We might, of course, ultimately reject our original value if it clearly produced highly undesirable consequences. But such an evaluation of desirability or undesirability in the consequences is a matter for opinion rather than scientific decision. Yet the investigation leading to that evaluation would be made according to scientific methods.

Actually, as Smith points out, a good deal of the fundamental research that is currently going on in the field of personality on how various personality characteristics function and what conditions produce them contributes to our understanding of mental health. For we can conceive of positive mental health as being made up of adjustive capacities and processes, many of which have long been of interest even to the psychologist who expresses little interest in evaluating adjustment.

For example, the ability to perceive reality accurately without distortion from needs is one personality characteristic whose origin and function is of continual concern in systematic personality research. Another example is independence in the face of pressures to conformity. In the Asch study on the influence of group pressures on perceptual judgments, which we have mentioned in other contexts earlier, some of the experimental subjects gave in to the pressure while others did not. Since the original studies were undertaken, researchers have been attempting first to ascertain the personality correlates of these degrees of dependence or independence of group sanction, and ultimately to determine the conditions of life that produce them. If such qualities are pertinent to positive mental health, we can understand their origin and function by doing research on them. Such basic personality research contributes to our understanding of mental health.

By stressing the well-adjusted person and the definition of pertinent qualities, we have taken an approach that is the reverse of the usual tendency in this field to begin with failures of adjustment. So strong in fact is this tendency to discuss mental health in terms of abnormal behavior that of late many psychologists have strongly criticized the traditional perspective on the problem. Still, the negative approach persists because the extreme instances of maladjustment are in some ways easier to sketch than are the characteristics of positive mental health. Now let us consider the problem of adjustive failure a bit more fully.

PSYCHOPATHOLOGY AS THE CLINICAL ASPECT OF MENTAL HEALTH

The problem of psychopathology, or adjustive failure, constitutes the subject matter of abnormal psychology. This field includes the description and analysis of the dynamics of the various forms of adjustive disturbances. These are the problems social workers, psychiatrists, and clinical psychologists deal with, by means of diagnosis and therapy, in the professional setting of clinic, hospital, or private practice. Psychopathology is usually linked to the concept of defense mechanism, and the various forms of mental disorder are, accordingly, thought to be based on the various kinds of ego-defensive maneuvers people employ. It will obviously be easier to understand the main forms of psychopathology—the neuroses, psychoses, and character disorders—if we first know something about these ego-defense mechanisms.

Ego-Defense Mechanisms

Defenses consist of special kinds of effort to cope with the psychological stress that arises from the conflicts between important demands. By resorting to a defense mechanism a person engages in self-deception about the nature of these conflicting demands, and in this way, appears to resolve the conflict and reduce the stress it produces. Self-deceptions, or defenses, are common, and they probably enable most people to live reasonably comfortable lives without having to continue to face problems that are too difficult to cope with more adaptively. For example, one way we deal with the inevitable prospect of dying is to avoid thinking or speaking about the subject most of the time. We may even find persons who are suffering from incurable cancer denying to themselves and others that they are dying and planning future activities as though they have a long life ahead. While this is often a heartbreaking self-deception to watch, it seems to ease the burden for the dying person.

A number of defense mechanisms have been postulated by Freud and later theorists, each of them involving different means by which a person protects himself. Let us examine a few examples of the most common.

Repression was originally to Freud the fundamental defense and all the others merely variations of it. Essentially, repression is the process whereby threatening, unacceptable, anxiety-producing urges and the ideas and feelings associated with these urges are restricted from a person's consciousness so that he is unaware of their existence. By this self-deception, he protects himself against the intolerable subjective danger and anxiety that would be generated if the impulse were permitted to express itself. In the related defense of *denial,* he may further distort the dangerous reality by a spirited disavowal of the impulse or the feelings and ideas related to it. Thus, a person may deny that he is angry, even when there are behavioral indications that he is, or aver that his child is not feeble-minded, even in the face of over-whelmingly strong evidence to the contrary.

Closely related to repression and denial is *reaction formation.* In this mechanism a person goes one step beyond denying an impulse and vigorously affirms its opposite. Thus, not only may he disclaim feeling angry toward someone, but he may also strongly declare his love. How effective a way this is to deceive onself, if not others, about the presence of an unacceptable impulse by parading before everyone feelings that are the opposite of what is true! "No, I am not angry, I love you." "No, I do not wish to be dependent upon you and to be taken care of as a child, I am really strong and independent and need no help." Incidentally, one of the favorite current hypotheses in psychosomatic medicine about the etiology of ulcers is related to this last illustration of reaction formation: An ulcer victim is often a hard-driving, hard-working, self-made man who is actually manifesting the opposite of powerful, chronic impulses toward dependency. The attitudes developed in reaction formation are usually considered to be continuous, to make up a pervasive and stable quality of the personality, whereas denial is a maneuver directed specifically at one event.

Another group of apparently related defense mechanisms includes intel-lectualization, isolation, and undoing. In *intellectualization* a person disen-gages himself from the emotional content of an experience or situation and examines it entirely from an intellectual point of view. It is a defense designed to deal with threats that originate externally. A magnificent example of such a mechanism in normal operation may be found in the experience of a student doctor. His first examination and partial dissection of a human corpse is a potentially terrifying experience, and an emotional reaction to it might well disqualify him from developing as a physician who must learn to approach human tissues, human suffering, and even death in a sufficiently detached fashion to protect himself against overinvolvement, which could render him useless in providing skilled medical services. Rather, the student must be capable of so disengaging himself emotionally from the situation that he regards a corpse, when he is in training, and a living human body, when he is in practice, intellectually, as he might in seeing a picture in a textbook.

Of course, certain conditions of medical practice make this task easier. For example, when a surgeon operates on a patient, most of the patient is covered with a sheet except for the particular area to be worked on, and to some degree this enables the doctor to maintain psychological distance from the patient. The patient in a hospital who complains of coldness and callousness on the part of nurses might well remember that if a nurse allowed herself to become overly involved emotionally with many of her patients, she would soon become deeply disturbed and unable to function. During her experience she probably learns to depend on this intellectualization process as a defense. But although this detachment protects her, a patient who wants more than merely mechanical sympathy may interpret it as frustrating disinterest.

In the defense mechanism of *isolation,* a person may separate two incompatible kinds of mental activity as a means of reducing conflict. This device is closely related to intellectualization since, in a sense, in intellectualization a person isolates, or separates, his emotional experience from his intellectual activity. In isolation a person may hold on to two entirely incompatible values, each kept apart from the other without distress. Toward his family a man may be kind and affectionate, whereas toward others he is ruthless and unyielding. The two patterns of experience remain isolated from one another, just as in intellectualization thinking and perceiving are kept separate from feelings.

Intimately related to intellectualization and isolation is the mechanism of *undoing,* in which a person attempts, by continual repetition of an impulse, feeling, or act, to negate it and control it. Instead of forgetting about a previously disturbing experience he may dream about it repetitiously, may ruminate about it, or recurrently re-examine it, as though repenting for wrongdoing and attempting to alleviate guilt and anxiety by repeating the act or thought in order to undo it. Only by facing it again and again and manipulating it somehow in an effort at "belated mastery" does the person feel he can control the situation.

Many more mechanisms of defense have been described than we have indicated. To elaborate the full catalog of such defenses would require far more space than would be justified here, but the reader is urged to explore fuller treatments of the theory of defense mechanisms elsewhere. A summary chart for ego-defense mechanisms, prepared for a text in abnormal psychology, is presented here in Table 1. It is somewhat oversimplified but gives a clear listing and description of a variety of defenses. We should also note that there is no universally agreed upon catalog of defenses. The area of ego-defense mechanisms is one in which we can learn a great deal more by systematic observation, experimentation, and theorizing.

Whether defense-mechanisms are good or bad is a matter of values, and, as we noted earlier, involves the same problem of judging as any kind of adjustment. But the extensive use of ego-defense mechanisms does have consequences for the individual that most observers consider damaging to mental health. For this reason, they typically regard the defenses as pathological, and each type of defense, when extreme, seems to be associated with a certain

TABLE 1

A Typical List of Ego-Defense Mechanisms

Mechanism	Function
Denial of reality	Protecting self from unpleasant reality by refusal to perceive it.
Fantasy	Gratifying frustrated desires in imaginary achievements.
Compensation	Covering up weaknesses by emphasizing desirable trait or making up for frustration in one area by overgratification in another.
Identification	Increasing feelings of worth by identifying with person or institution of illustrious standing.
Introjection	Incorporating external values and standards into ego structure so individual is not at their mercy as external threats.
Projection	Placing blame for difficulties upon others or attributing one's own unethical desires to others.
Rationalization	Attempting to prove that one's behavior is "rational" and justifiable and thus worthy of self and social approval.
Repression	Preventing painful or dangerous thoughts from entering consciousness.
Reaction formation	Preventing dangerous desires from being expressed by exaggerating opposed attitudes and types of behavior and using them as "barriers."
Displacement	Discharging pent-up feelings, usually of hostility, on objects less dangerous than those which initially aroused the emotions.
Emotional insulation	Withdrawing into passivity to protect self from hurt.
Isolation	Cutting off affective charge from hurtful situations or separating incompatible attitudes by logic-tight compartments.
Regression	Retreating to earlier developmental level involving less mature responses and usually a lower level of aspiration.
Sublimation	Gratifying frustrated sexual desires in substitute nonsexual activities.
Undoing	Atoning for and thus counteracting immoral desires and acts.

From Coleman, J. C., *Abnormal psychology and modern life.* Chicago: Scott, Foresman, 1950, p. 95.

pattern of psychopathological symptoms. In our discussion of the types of psychopathology, we can only touch lightly on the description and dynamics of different disturbances, but the reader is encouraged to use other sources that offer a fuller treatment.

Adequacy
of Adjustment
and the
Problem of
Mental Health

As we have said, each form of adjustive failure represents a different way of dealing with conflict and its consequent psychological stress, and the symptoms are reflections of these methods of defense as observed in personal behavior. The main forms of psychopathology are neuroses, psychoses, and character disorders. Let us consider each briefly.

The Neuroses.   The neurotic person deceives himself about conflicting demands, but the ego-defensive activity that produces this distortion of reality is either too ineffective to succeed fully, or it results in further difficulties. In the *anxiety neuroses,* the defense, whatever it is, is inadquate, and chronic uneasiness and occasional acute panic is the predominant complaint. The anxiety is sometimes expressed in psychosomatic disorders, in the symptoms of insomnia, "nervousness," difficulties in concentrating, or fatigue or exhaustion (called asthenia); sometimes in special irrational fears (called phobias); and sometimes in unreasonable preoccupation with bodily health and imaginary symptoms (called hypochondria).

Strong repression and related defense-mechanisms are thought to underlie the neurotic disorder known as *hysteria,* producing such symptoms as loss of memory (amnesia), loss of sensation or paralysis (conversion reactions), or dissociative states which include fugues, sleepwalking, and multiple personalities. In a fugue, the person forgets who he is and may wander or travel (fugue means flight) to some other place, establishing a new life and identity which may last many years. In the disorder known as multiple personality, as was portrayed in the popular book and motion picture "The Three Faces of Eve," the person appears to alternate among several personalities, as though each were a separate entity.

Compulsions and *obsessions* are the result of the defense-mechanisms of isolation and undoing. In these conditions a person feels compelled against his will to engage in strange rituals that are alien to him (isolation), such as constantly washing his hands (compulsion), or to think certain seemingly irrational thoughts (obsessions), such as having been sinful or being certain that he will hurt someone he loves. The defense of undoing represents, in compulsions, efforts to "undo" real or imagined acts of which he is ashamed, as when Shakespeare's Lady Macbeth attempted to undo the murder of King Duncan by symbolically washing his blood off her hands over and over again. The theory of defense is, in fact, an explanatory statement about all the forms of neurosis.

The Psychoses.   Whereas neuroses vary in degree of severity, but are rarely so incapacitating as to lead to hospitalization, psychoses are the most severe form of psychopathology, commonly requiring community efforts to treat afflicted persons. In common psychological opinion, the psychotic person is someone who is failing to manage, or successfully defend against, threatening or socially unacceptable impulses. The personality becomes severely disorganized in consequence and the threatening impulses may "break through" into behavior. When this happens, the psychotic appears to lose his normal behavioral controls and is apt to frighten or offend people who do not understand his predicament. Sometimes he is actually dangerous to himself and others.

As with neurosis, the forms of the disorders reflect the particular adjustment mechanisms commonly used to deal with life's stresses. Only, in the case of the psychotic, there seems to be a severe breakdown of normal adult or neurotic adjustment patterns. The adjustments appear to be primitive, and often child-like, and the term "regression" is often used to refer to this disorganization of personality processes. At one time the psychotic person was presumably able to use more mature forms of adjustment, but, either because of unusually severe stress or because of faulty childhood experience that led to fragile or easily overwhelmed mechanisms of adjustment, he regresses to more inadequate levels of coping with life's demands.

There are many forms of psychosis, the most serious and perplexing being the *schizophrenic disorders*. These involve disturbances of the normal thought processes, bizarre patterns of behavior, and psychological withdrawal from social relations into a private world of hallucination and delusion. In the most severely regressed forms, such as hebephrenia and catatonia, the schizophrenic individual must be cared for, since he may be incontinent and unable to make even the simplest adaptive efforts to care for himself.

Paranoia, depression, and *mania* are other forms of psychosis. A person in the first-named state manifests mainly delusions of persecution or of grandeur. He may consider himself in danger of being attacked by others, or he may believe he is some famous person such as Jesus Christ or Napoleon. In depression, there are deep feelings of hopelessness and guilt, often so profound that a person may attempt suicide during a depressive attack. There is a continuum in the depth of depression, from "normal" sadness, or blueness, to the more severe neurotic and the even deeper psychotic depressions. In psychotic depression the person requires hospitalization and continued care for the duration of the disturbance. Manic attacks, which may alternate with depressive periods in some persons, are another form of "affective disorder." In mania, a person enters a period of euphoria and excitement that may make him a nuisance, cause him to be difficult to manage, and disturb his judgment about the conduct of his affairs.

The Character Disorders.   We might best regard the character disorders also as stemming from failure to acquire normal mechanisms of behavioral control. In the usual case there is a chronic problem of excessive, impulsive self-indulgence that defeats the person's effectiveness in mastering the social circumstances of his life. He does not usually suffer from the conflict-produced anxiety that burdens and inhibits the neurotic and leads to a breakdown of controls in the psychotic. Rather, he is inadequate to the ordinary tasks of living. As a consequence of faulty personality development, he often has a history of social and occupational failure and of getting into continual trouble with the law. He may attempt to solve problems that are common to everyone by resorting to drugs or alcohol. In other instances, he may perpetually seek a dependent relationship with others, as in the passive-dependent personality, or lash out at them when frustrated, as in the aggressive personality who cannot seem to control his anger and impulsively discharges it without restraint. Each type of character disorder reflects the behavioral consequences of a particular way of meeting problems of living.

Our aim in these past few pages has been to throw into relief the problem of maladjustment. But admittedly we have provided only the most sketchy coverage of a rich area of theory and observation. There are, of course, other general classes of adjustive failure that we have not dealt with. For example, *organic psychoses* and *mental deficiency* are instances of failure to adjust successfully to stress and conflict because of an inadequately functioning or damaged central nervous system. Moreover, we could have cited more than one viewpoint about the causes and dynamics of the psychopathologies. As we shall see in Chapter 6, alternative theories of personality exist, and these theories often disagree about the bases of adjustive failure. Here, we have tied the various disorders to types of ego-defenses. And although this represents perhaps the most widely held general view among clinical workers today, it is only one point of view. Clearly, we still need to learn much about the nature and dynamics of psychopathology and its relationship to healthy personality.

Up to now we have discussed adjustment in terms of the external and internal demands that require it and the conflict between these demands, and we have considered the problem of evaluating adjustment and psychopathology. But there is another way of approaching adjustment, one that requires no evaluation at all but merely focuses on the processes involved—that is, on *how* an individual adjusts rather than *how well*. From this point of view we are not obliged to judge adjustive adequacy, but only to study, describe, and understand a person's efforts to cope with his environment.

Already, in fact, when we briefly discussed forms of adjustment such as accommodation or assimilation and when we alluded to defense mechanisms, we were approaching *adjustment as a process* rather than as an end result that an individual successfully or unsuccessfully accomplishes. We may take this line of inquiry without any practical intent other than to understand.

When we attempt to understand the processes of adjustment, how they work, and how they develop, we clearly enter the realm of the psychology of personality. We are no longer interested solely in momentary efforts to adjust to particular conditions, but in the over-all stable patterns of adjustment and their determinants. When we conceive of adjustment in this way—that is, as stable processes—we have entered the field of personality proper.

What
Personality Is

The sources of man's be-
havior (his observable action) and his subjective experience (such as thoughts, feelings, and wishes) are twofold:
the external stimuli that impinge on him and the internal
dispositions that result from the interaction between
inherited physiological characteristics and experience with
the world. When we focus on the former, we note that a
person acts in such-and-such a way because of certain
qualities in a situation. For example, he attacks a friend
because the friend insulted him, or he loses interest in a
lecture because the teacher is dull or uninformed, or he
fails in his program of study because the necessity of

27

3

supporting himself through school leaves insufficient time for studying. It is evident that a man's behavior varies greatly from moment to moment, from circumstance to circumstance, changing with the changing conditions to which he is exposed.

Still, even as we recognize the dependency of behavior on outside stimuli, we are also aware that it cannot be accounted for on the basis of the external situation alone, but that in fact it must arise partly from personal characteristics. For example, the same quantity of alcohol that will induce loss of control and dilapidated behavior in one individual will produce scarcely noticeable effects in another. Some of this variation, of course, can be laid to momentary physical and social conditions. For instance, when the social circumstances of drinking are friendly and benign, a person may be less guarded and more inclined to permit himself to get drunk than when the situation is hostile or dangerous. Moreover, the amount and type of food in the stomach before and during drinking also determine the alcoholic effect by influencing the rate of absorption of the alcohol into the bloodstream and its subsequent effects on the brain.

But some of the variations in the effects of alcohol or any other stimulus result from stable personal characteristics that are almost always in operation in all situations. Body weight, for example, is quite influential in determining the physiological and psychological effects given quantities of alcohol can produce. Then too, psychologically, some persons are more concerned than others with exercising controls or restraints over behavior, so they keep the lid on the dilapidating and disinhibiting effects of alcohol, sometimes even until they lose consciousness or go to sleep. But other personality characteristics can lead a person to lose control very rapidly and grow either depressed, unruly, and hostile, or exceedingly sociable and outgoing. Or, to take a non-alcoholic example, one person may virtually never get discouraged and give up trying to accomplish something even when the circumstances warrant it, while another quits trying at the first evidence of trouble.

It is certain that a person's behavior is governed not only by momentary external stimulation, but also by the stable attributes he carries about with him. Clearly, then, we must identify these attributes, or dispositions, if we are to understand and predict psychological reactions. For these attributes are what we mean by personality. And the identifiable reactions are the end result of the interplay between them and immediate situations. In short, both external stimuli and personality must be taken into account in understanding and predicting human behavior and subjective experience.

PERSONALITY AS AN INFERRED THEORETICAL CONSTRUCT

When a layman says that someone "has a good personality," he is making a value judgment. Different observers, however, are likely to make different judgments about the same personality depending on what they find appealing in another person. The psychologist, in contrast, means by personality certain determining qualities that are reflected in behavior. The term has a scientific meaning independent of any value judgments that might be made about how nice or desirable someone is as a friend, spouse, or colleague. As we shall see later on in this volume, scientific personality assessment involves describing a person as he is rather than evaluating him by our private standards of what is desirable or undesirable.

In describing the personalities of people, psychologists use the concepts of structure and process. Structures are the more or less stable arrangements of parts in a system, whereas processes have to do with the functions carried out by the parts, what they do, and how they interact and change. The geological patterns of the countryside about us are *structures* because the individual parts—hills, river beds, even the foliage—are relatively stable or semi-permanent fixtures of the area, recognizable to us as familiar objects and patterns. If we wish to describe the area geologically, we will refer to these objects and patterns.

Still, even though there are stable aspects or structures, we must remember that these structures evolved out of continuing, interacting forces over time, and that these forces are still operating to slowly alter the very features that appear to us, in our limited time-span, as fixed. Thus, wind, the flow of water down the river beds from the mountain watersheds, the effects of storms—all these and many more conditions are producing changes in the structures, just as the structures of the valleys themselves determine how fast and in what direction the river water will flow, and just as the hills affect the wind direction and velocity. These changes and the interplay of natural environmental forces are *processes.* Any system is described by the scientist in terms of structures and processes. Thus, we can speak of social structures (for instance, our cultural institutions) and social processes (such as the interplay among groups of people, and the effects of institutions on human activity), and of biological structures (say, tissue or organ systems) and biological processes (for example, metabolism, or cell death and replacement).

Many of the structures and processes in the physical, biological, and social sciences are not directly observable and must be constructed by theoretical effort. For example, the oxidation of food or metals is a process we cannot see, but we know about it from observing the regular changes that occur under given conditions of temperature when these substances are exposed to oxygen. The atom comprises a structure with parts or substructures that have never been seen directly yet they interact in certain clearly discernible processes. We know about these theoretically conceived structures and processes from carefully controlled observations of the conditions under which they occur and the effects they produce.

In the same way, psychological structures and processes are theoretical constructs that we cannot directly observe, though we try to learn about them by inference from their conditions and effects. Thus, mental abilities are not observable but their effects are. The person who has much ability presumably will solve problems better, or display more information, than someone with less ability. We cannot measure the ability directly but we can know about it from the results of tests. Similarly, a need is a theoretically derived structure and reduction or elimination of need-tensions are theoretically inferred processes (sometimes referred to by psychologists as dynamics).

We must emphasize that the psychologist of personality does not identify personality simply by a person's actions, noting, for example, dominant or passive behavior. He is concerned with the structures and processes that bring about the superficial behavior that he observes. It is these determinants that we are trying to identify and describe, particularly the stable ones as opposed to transient characteristics that come and go. The essence of the problem is that we can observe only superficial behavior, which consists of motor acts, verbal statements, gestures or expressive movements, and a few physiological events that have visible consequences—for example, blushing, growing pale, and sweating. So the task of identifying the personality structures that cause behavior is most challenging precisely because those structures are not directly observable. Personality is, therefore, an inference or a set of inferences we make about a person from direct observation of his behavior.

In other words, when we observe people behaving in particular ways in various situations, again and again we find consistent patterns. Such consistent patterns imply the presence of certain personality structures and processes that determine them. The scientist of personality must speculate about the personality system, reconstructing theoretically what must be involved in order to make sense out of what he has observed. This speculation is a creative act of scientific imagination. We shall have more to say systematically about the construction and evaluation of personality theory as we proceed further.

BEHAVIORAL EVIDENCE
OF PERSONALITY STRUCTURE AND PROCESS

The human behavior that permits us to make inferences about personality structure takes a number of diverse forms. One is *directed action* from which we can interpret motivations. For example, take two students: One spends the bulk of his time studying whereas the other passes his time in social activities. What do their choices of behavior between two alternatives suggest about their underlying motives? We might infer that the first student is directed principally toward academic achievement and that the second has a strong affiliation need (the wish to be liked and accepted by others). And we might support our inferences by information from other sources, such as personal introspection on the part of the student. But when we have such additional information, we might have to revise our original inferences. The first student, for instance, may tell us that, although he really has strong affiliative urges, he studies a great deal because social interaction frightens him.

When we are dealing with organisms other than man, we are especially dependent on *expressive movements,* or posture, in making inferences about motivational and emotional states. Thus, we learn to recognize anger in the snarl and arched back of a dog or cat, and we may note cringing and defecation as evidence of a strong state of fear. For people as well, styles of action and gestures are useful sources of information about inner psychological events, and we often rely on them especially to identify moods and emotional states.

In man, verbal language provides still another key to inner experience and to the character of personality structure and dynamics. It is the means by which he can *introspect,* label his experiences, and report them to an observer. For one thing, an observer himself may introspect about his own reactions in the situations his subject is in and report verbally on it. For example, when we observe a person who has recently lost through death someone he deeply loved, by means of empathy we are likely to infer that he is experiencing grief because we ourselves have that feeling in a similar situation. The success of this kind of interpretation and inference depends, however, on similarities among people, and it is highly subject to error because individual differences also exist among people in the impact of identical situations. Thus, one person may experience primarily grief, another gratification and guilt, and a third relative indifference. Because of these differences, interpretations based on *empathic introspection* by the observer are hazardous.

Language can provide another introspective source of information about personality characteristics. By means of the *introspection of the person being studied* we may learn a great deal about what he is thinking, feeling, and wishing. We may ask him to tell us about these things and, to the degree that he is willing and able to identify and express them, he provides information about his inner experience and the structure of his personality.

Special problems arise in using such verbal reports in making inferences about personality structure, for words can be used to dissimulate as well as to communicate. That is, a person may employ speech to express what he wishes another person to believe rather than what is actually true. Thus, if we take the introspection at face value, we may interpret it incorrectly. We may miss the fact, for example, that an individual has angry feelings about someone else even though he denies that he does. To a degree, of course, the same problem exists for motor behavior, since a person can also create various impressions on an observer by his motor actions. But the nuances and richness of language make the problem of deception especially acute in the case of introspection.

Despite this drawback, a great deal of our knowledge about psychodynamics arises from careful analysis of introspections, especially during psychotherapy (which is thus not only a treatment method but an important source of information about personality). But psychotherapy requires a sophisticated interpretation of introspection, for the therapist cannot usually accept at face value what the client says about his feelings. Rather, he continually checks his interpretations against other behavioral sources of information and against other statements the client has made over a long period. Thus, by comparing introspections from time to time and from situation to situation, it is possible to improve on the validity of interpretations about personality structure and dynamics.

In recent years another behavioral source of information has gained prominence as a systematic method of inferring personality characteristics—*physiological manifestations* of emotional states. Some of the physiological concomitants to emotion, which have been known in a rough way for a long time, can be observed and interpreted without technically advanced instruments. For example, flushing and paling of the face signify internal disturbances that are associated with, respectively, anger and fear. The physiological reason for such color changes is that, in emotional states, certain types of activity occur in the autonomic nervous system and in the hormonal secretions of the body. Nowadays we have electronic instruments that, by measuring rapid and minute changes in reactivity of the autonomic nervous system and in body chemistry, enable us to identify emotional arousal in a person more accurately. An example of measurement of the autonomic nervous system in experimental research on psychological stress is shown in Figure 1. A film that contained disturbing scenes was presented to a large number of subjects, and the electrical conductivity of the skin was continuously recorded for each subject during the film. The points of stress for the group are evident in the peak reactions in the graph. Because of such technical advances, psychophysiological methods are of increasing value in the assessment of personality structure and dynamics.

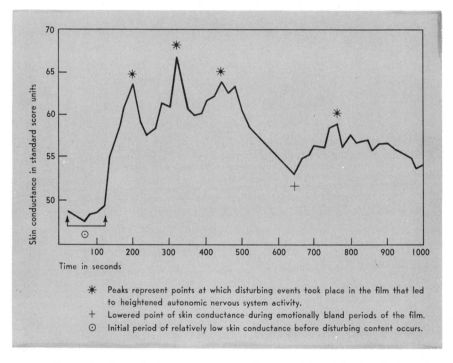

* Peaks represent points at which disturbing events took place in the film that led to heightened autonomic nervous system activity.
+ Lowered point of skin conductance during emotionally bland periods of the film.
⊙ Initial period of relatively low skin conductance before disturbing content occurs.

Figure 1. Record of average changes (for 68 subjects) in electrical conductivity of the skin in response to an emotionally disturbing motion picture. (Adapted from Lazarus, R. S.; Speisman, J. C.; and Mordkoff, A. M. The relationship between autonomic indicators of psychological stress: heart rate and skin conductance. Psychosom. Med., in press.)

A key point in the consideration of these various behavioral sources of information about personality is this: They do not always lead to the same inference about personality structure and dynamics. Indeed, we often find what on the surface appear to be contradictions among them. Thus, someone may state that he is not angry, although he flushes, develops migraine headaches, or acts destructively toward others—clear signs of anger.

If we try to make inferences about personality structure from only one aspect of behavior we are likely to make frequent errors. The reason for error probably lies in the complex organization of personality, which can be fully known only through its multitude of behavioral manifestations. This is especially true when we are dealing with strong conflict and emotional states, because these often elicit ego-defense mechanisms. Since an individual may be literally unaware of certain impulses and feelings in himself, he cannot communicate them by introspection. So an observer must check one source against another in making his interpretation in order to uncover defense mechanisms and take them into account. Clearly, the task of making inferences about personality characteristics is subtle and hazardous. Personality assessment, which we shall discuss later, is concerned with precisely this problem: translating behavior into valid and useful inferences about personality structure and dynamics.

Implicit in our discussion so far has been an important distinction: that between *surface and depth in personality*. The concept of defense mechanism implies that surface behavior often conceals certain personality characteristics, and that recognizing them would be unfortunate for a person. For example, beneath surface aggression may be unexpressed, even unrecognized, fear. To understand the surface aggression properly we must recognize the hidden fear that generates it and which is deep within the personality. It is deep because it represents the unseen causal processes that cannot be directly known in contrast to the surface, which is directly observable.

The term depth carries on the famous physical analogy Freud employed to distinguish between what we directly observe in behavior and what we infer or conceptualize theoretically as the determining structures and processes (see Figure 2). The analogy is to an iceberg, which reveals on the surface of the water only a small portion of its total mass, the rest being sunk beneath the sea and invisible unless we seek it out. This is a vivid way of dramatizing the distinction between those psychological events that are empirically observable and those that are not. Because we often act in ways we do not understand, ways that involve psychological processes we cannot identify, the word "depth," in personality theory, has also come to signify, for many, unconsciousness. The idea is, what is deep is inaccessible to us and therefore occurs without our awareness. But the distinction between consciousness and unconsciousness is controversial in psychology. Many academic psychologists tend to distrust speculation without clear evidence of the existence of the theoretically conceived processes. But among psychologists of personality, especially in the applied fields of clinical psychology and psychiatry, as well as among literate lay persons, the concept of unconscious processes has had wide acceptance and usage. In any event, we can know the structure and dynamics of personality, with or without the notion of unconsciousness, only by the speculative processes, of theory construction and inference.

THE EVALUATION OF PERSONALITY THEORY

We have been discussing in the preceding section *theoretical statements* about the psychology of personality. We identified them as speculations about structures and processes in order to distinguish them from *empirical statements* about relationships between observable events, such as introspec-

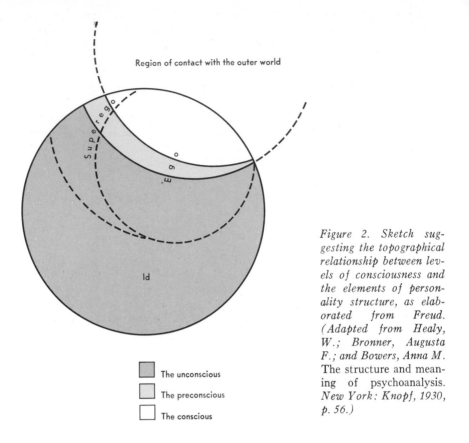

Region of contact with the outer world

Superego

Ego

Id

The unconscious

The preconscious

The conscious

Figure 2. Sketch suggesting the topographical relationship between levels of consciousness and the elements of personality structure, as elaborated from Freud. (Adapted from Healy, W.; Bronner, Augusta F.; and Bowers, Anna M. The structure and meaning of psychoanalysis. New York: Knopf, 1930, p. 56.)

tive reports and other behavioral acts. The science of personality encompasses both kinds of statements. Empirical statements can always be tested directly, since they consist only of relationships among observable acts. For example, we can directly assess the validity of the statement that people who score high on certain tests of intelligence are more likely to have good grades in school. But a theoretical explanation of this in terms of concepts of intelligence cannot be directly tested, since we cannot witness intelligence itself. As a theoretical construct it must be inferred from what is observable.

Still, in science, it is necessary to test or evaluate our theoretical statements to determine which ones are accurate and useful models of structure and process. We make such an evaluation by deducing certain new empirical relationships. That is, we make "if . . . then . . ." statements based on our theoretical formulations. If such-and-such a system applies, then we should be able to observe its appropriate empirical consequences. Since these consequences deal with observable behavior, the deduced relationships can be directly tested. If the relationship does not hold in fact, then we must either discard or revise our theoretical model.

The task of evaluating theory is a vast and complex one. The process of constructing theoretical systems is always going on, and the discovery of empirical facts proceeds hand in hand with it. Many different theories are actually possible, the number being limited only by scientists' ingenuity and scope of knowledge. In young fields like the psychology of personality many theoretical systems have been created, involving various assumptions about the psychological construction and functioning of man. The presence of many systems means, of course, that we do not at present know enough to evaluate them definitively and discard the less adequate conceptions in favor of more useful models.

Actually, many of the theoretical systems in personality share a great deal in common in the way of postulated structures and processes. So, we shall consider in the next chapter some of the basic qualities and structures of personality that most theorists regard as fundamental and which they incorporate in their theories in one form or another. Later on we shall look at the differences among theoretical positions.

Fundamental Qualities and Structures of Personality

So far, we have not articulated the details of what we mean by personality. We have talked about it, especially about the process of inference, and the behavioral evidence from which the inference is made. But we need to consider more directly what personality is. We shall now do so under two headings. In the first section we shall take up the fundamental qualities, which include consistency, development of structure, potentiality for change, and integration. The second section covers two specific typical personality constructs, motivation and control.

36

4

Consistency

One hallmark of person-
ality is consistency, or stability. If we had no consistent personal qualities,
we could not conceive of personality, since we would all be continually changing so much that we would scarcely be recognizable. People are the same
in many ways over long periods of time. Thus, when we enter a classroom,
we expect to be able to recognize the instructor time and time again without
difficulty, even though his clothing has changed, his mood is different, or his
lecture materials are altered. His body contours, general size, and the physical features of his face and other visible portions of his body constitute a
stable physical structure that remains constant throughout most of his adult
life. Just like physical structure, personality structure exhibits consistency.
A person is recognizable from situation to situation by the consistent qualities
of personality that are reflected in his behavior.

Not that he acts exactly the same way in every situation. We know this
is simply not true. In fact, some years ago two psychologists, Hartshorne and
May, undertook an outstanding series of studies to determine the consistency of moral behavior. They attacked the question of whether honest behavior reflects stable attributes of character. (Actually, in keeping with the
emphasis of the times when they did their studies, the authors took the position that we can speak only of honest or dishonest acts in particular situations, because underlying character structure does not exist.) By means of
ingenious tests they studied a large number of preadolescent children under a
variety of circumstances that permitted them to act honestly or dishonestly.
In one instance, for example, cheating in a classroom test was investigated by
returning the tests to the children and asking them to grade their own papers.
The teacher read aloud the correct answers and the children scored their
papers without knowing that a wax impression was made of their original
answers. Since some tests were in the classroom, some in the home setting,
and some on the athletic field, the authors could determine to what extent
specific setting—as opposed to consistent traits of character—determined
degree of honest behavior.

Hartshorne and May found little consistency in degree of honesty. A few
children were usually honest and a few usually dishonest, but most varied appreciably depending on circumstances. As a consequence of these findings the
authors argued that honesty is not a trait of character. People only act
honestly or dishonestly in reaction to particular situations.

In the ensuing years many criticisms were leveled against these studies,
not so much against the methodology as against the conclusions drawn from
them. When Hartshorne and May did their research, academic psychologists
were less inclined than today to think in terms of hypothetical constructs of
personality, and the major emphasis then was on overt behavior and its description rather than on unifying processes. The Freudian revolution in personality theory had not yet had its full impact on academic psychology, so
Hartshorne and May thought of consistency of personality or character in
terms of directly observable behavior. They asked only whether honest or

dishonest behavior would be repeated from situation to situation. They did not consider psychological factors within the person that might determine the behavior.

One of their little-noticed findings, for example, was that bright children cheated less than dull children. Perhaps they had less reason: because they knew their work and were confident of doing well they could afford not to cheat, and indeed may have even had fewer opportunities. It is probable, too, that the children's desire to succeed varied with each particular test or circumstance. For instance, one child might urgently want to be regarded as the best athlete in the class, thereby implying a strong motivation to do well in athletics. Such a child, when permitted to misjudge without fear of detection the length of a broad jump, might readily add an inch or two if it meant gaining prestige among other children. This same child, however, might have far less motivation to distinguish himself in English grammar or arithmetic, in which case the likelihood of cheating would be reduced. In short, the consistency to look for might not be at the level of simple behavioral acts, but rather in the determining structures and processes of personality, such as motivation. The fundamental difficulty with the conclusions of Hartshorne and May is that their definition of consistency was couched entirely in terms of behavioral acts rather than of inferred personality structure on which the acts must rest.

The Hartshorne and May studies are prime examples of a current that is no longer in the main stream of thought about personality. We are not interested today merely in simple behavioral acts, even though our inferences about stable personality structures and processes must derive from observations of behavior. We now view consistency in the context of the larger aspects of human behavior. For example, the specific acts that I perform in writing this manuscript vary with the conditions under which I must write, so that the detailed movements I make in typing a page give way to entirely different acts when I dictate the passage and let the secretary perform the task of pressing the correct typewriter keys. These details of motor acts are sometimes referred to as *molecular* events in contrast with more *molar* types of analyses, so that, although the specific motor acts differ, there are recognizable features to my style of writing, the attitudes reflected in its content, and the unseen intentions (motives) that lie behind the activity. We recognize the stability of these latter, more molar properties of the individual even when particular motor acts change. It is usually irrelevant whether I type a passage, write it by hand, or dictate it into a recorder. For most purposes, the significant aspects of personality in these acts are the stable motives, skills, and knowledge involved in their performance; and these must be inferred from observation of superficial consistencies as well as inconsistencies in the style and content of the activity.

The modern science of personality thus puts more stress on a type of behavioral consistency we can sum up as styles of action—what researchers have called *expressive movements* because they may express certain underlying organizing qualities of personality. Here the spotlight is turned on the form that any intentional act can take—its style of expression. For example, artists are easily recognized by their personal styles, regardless of the subject of the particular painting or where the work was done. Particular acts may not distinguish two individuals or the same individual under different conditions, but the style, or form, of expression of acts may well serve to identify a person.

Here are some of the styles, or expressive movements, that have been identified: the tempo, or speed, of action (for example, in the normal rate of handwriting); spatial aspects (for example, writing letters in a large and expansive, or small and cramped, way); and degree of emphasis (such as how lightly or heavily we bear down on a pen or pencil when we write or whether our gestures are definite and strong or uncertain and delicate). As anticipated, we find some consistency in the expressive movements a person would execute from time to time and from circumstance to circumstance. For example, a person's tempo of walking on a given occasion is related to his tempo of handwriting, as well as to his walking speed on other occasions. The closer in time and the nearer in quality the circumstances under which we study two expressive acts, the more consistency we can demonstrate.

The matter of expressive movements was one of the forerunners in research of modern interest in what has been recently called *cognitive styles*. Cognitive styles are ways of thinking and perceiving that characterize a person independently of the content of an act. They are therefore close cousins to expressive movements, except that they concern, instead of motor acts, cognitive processes like perception and thought. Thus, some persons, regardless of circumstances, have a tendency in their perceptual judgments and symbolic manipulations to overlook similarities and accentuate differences. These persons might be called sharpeners. In contrast, others—levelers— have a greater tendency to overlook differences and stress similarities. Because of such well-established tendencies, or cognitive structures, different persons approach the world and think about it in considerably different ways. Personologists interested in cognitive styles seek to identify such consistencies in the various fields of cognition, and to determine how the structures develop and how they influence a person's transactions with his environment.

Even when there is little or no consistency at the level of behavioral acts, there may be great stability or consistency in the hypothetical structures and processes that determine these surface acts. To borrow an attractive expression from theorist Kurt Lewin, "the same heat that melts the butter hardens the egg." The same structure, when reflected in different circumstances, may have superficially different, even opposite, effects. This kind of consistency of determining structures and processes is of the utmost importance in personality theory. As we shall see shortly, these determining structures and processes include motives and ways of expressing them and of coping with stress-producing conflicts.

If consistency is a basic characteristic of personality, what are its limitations? Does a high degree of consistency lead to an undesirable kind of fixity or rigidity? In fact, it may so reduce the plasticity of personality structure and the possibilities for its reorganization that a person can no longer successfully adapt to a changing milieu. Good examples of this point are common among elderly persons whose personalities (including internalized social values, roles, and ways of doing things) have become more and more ossified and unchangeable. Older people, of course, usually find themselves in a changing world, somewhat left behind, along with their most cherished values. New types of behavior or forms of adjustment are required of them, but often, because of the degree to which their personality structures have become rigid or set, they can no longer make this shift as can the younger, more flexible members of the society. Thus we see that stability of personality structure can be a disadvantage when reorganizations are called for and, furthermore, that excessive stability of structure is likely to be a characteristic of later life.

The Development of Personality Structure

In the view of many developmentally oriented psychologists, the growth of an organism proceeds from simple to increasingly complex structure from birth onward. When an infant begins life, according to developmental theorist Heinz Werner, his mental organization is diffuse and relatively limited. With passing time (which provides the opportunity for the maturation of genetic influences and the effects of experience), the child differentiates perceptually among the various features of his environment; thus, he becomes capable of distinguishing between himself and others and among the various significant persons around him. Ways of viewing the world and patterns of thought become crystallized, and the various facets of the child's experience become differentiated from one another as separate parts of his total mental structure. Ultimately these differentiated parts become integrated, or organized functionally.

In the development of perception, for example, a person becomes increasingly capable of observing some complex aspect of his environment, analyzing it into its component parts, and rapidly reorganizing those parts into an integrated whole. Thus, at this highest perceptual level of integration, we can apprehend another person not merely as a collection of unrelated physical features, such as fingers, hands, arms, legs, torso, and face, but as an organized system. We have merged the parts within a total concept—a person. The child passes, then, from apprehending the world as global and diffuse, through an analytic stage of progressive differentiation of the various components of the environment, to the level of synthesis, or integration, where he brings the parts together. The elements of his mental apparatus have progressively increased in number, in articulation, and in complexity of interrelationship. Psychologist Kurt Lewin has diagramed this progression of increasing structure as in Figure 3.

The reader may notice that this evolutionary conception of mental structure resembles the evolutionary conception of development in embryology. We can clearly trace through all phylogenetic levels a continuous development from single-cell stage—the fertilized egg—to complex organism. The fertilized egg is an extremely limited and simple structure, but the potentialities for cell differentiation along the lines inherent in the species are present in the genes of the cell nucleus. Inherent chemical activators stimulate differentiation into many groups of tissues with independent structures and functions. Eventually, in the mature organism, these separate tissue systems (for example, nervous tissue, skin tissue, and digestive tissue) operate in a unified way so that each contributes to the functioning and survival of the total organism. Developmental psychologists like to use this embryological pattern as an analogy for psychological development.

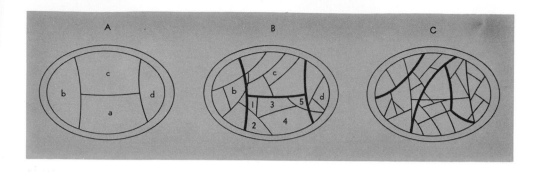

Figure 3. Lewin's topological representation of the increasing differentiation of psychological structure in development. (A) is the relatively undifferentiated state of early development. The whole system representing the person's psychological structure has relatively few parts. Regions a, b, c, and d could represent systems of needs, means of satisfying them, and other stable features of the structure. Lines separate these regions, their thickness indicating the extent of psychological independence between them. (B) represents a later stage of development in the same individual. There has been further differentiation into subregions. (C) is a further stage of development, with still more differentiation of parts and some changes in the basic structure. The newer regions show increasing implications in the motivational, emotional, and cognitive aspects of the personality. (Adapted from Lewin, K. Principles of topological psychology. *New York: McGraw-Hill, 1936, p. 190.)*

In studying the development of personality, we deal of course with hypothetical structures, including motivation and various patterns of regulation, or control, constructs that we shall talk about shortly. The point we want to make now is that, in addition to the primary, physiological motives that a person has at birth or that appear with neurological maturation, his life history includes the emergence and organization of many diverse motive patterns and values, each of which has some identity of its own, even though its operation is subordinated to an organic totality. Thus, the stable, consistently functioning structures of personality come into being in the process of development and, once formed, tend to resist modification.

Potentiality for Change

Although the concept of personality depends on the existence of stable component structures, observation of human behavior requires that we make theoretical room for the possibility of reorganizing those structures. In short, some degree of changeability must be present, as well as consistency.

Theories differ not only about how fixed or changeable personality is, but also about how early in life its basic structure is formed and stabilized. In the early 1900's psychologists turned their attention toward early childhood as the critical period in the establishment of personality structure. This emphasis on early childhood has often been regarded as one of Freud's major contributions to psychological thought. But today, many theorists, while agreeing with this judgment, feel that Freud was extreme in his emphasis. Freudian psychoanalysis seems to affirm that the essential elements of personality have already become firmly established within the first five years of life. In fact, in traditional Freudian therapy, analysis is not considered successful unless a patient's life from one to five has been thoroughly explored. From this point of view, only such exploration will enable a reorganization of adult personality structure. The view of orthodox psychoanalytic theorists is that, normally, relatively little that happens after these early years can alter the fundamental organization of the personality, with the possible exception of psychoanalytic treatment or severe, prolonged crises.

Many of the early disciples of Freud who later came to make up a diverse group of theorists known as the Neo-Freudians have been critical of Freud's stress on the early establishment of a fixed personality structure. They have re-emphasized the importance of later experiences in shaping personality, arguing that personality structure is not nearly so set in the early years as Freud had suggested. In the practice of psychotherapy, Neo-Freudians such as Karen Horney are concerned less with discovering and working out infantile experiences than with the nature and significance of a patient's current adjustive efforts. Without denying that these adjustive processes have early origins, they focus on how those processes currently function for the individual. The assumption is that a person retains his adjustive processes because they have some current value in reducing anxiety and increasing his sense of safety and security. Neo-Freudians further hold that many important traumatic and corrective experiences can occur relatively late in life.

Actually both points of view are valid, and they are not so contradictory as they might appear. From some recent developmental studies of persons from childhood to adulthood, it has become increasingly apparent that substantial changes in personality do indeed take place during adolescence and early adulthood. What is ambiguous is which personality structures are formed and fully established early in life and how they function or alter later in life. Is it not possible, though, that many aspects of personality can become highly stable during pre-adolescence and be retained throughout life, while still leaving room for the acquisition of new characteristics and for some, even if slight, reorganization of the old?

For example, suppose we have a chance to observe someone in pre-adolescence and again at the age of 30. As a child he is inadequate and anxious and deals with his problems by compulsive adherence to certain forms or rituals. Yet at 30 he has acquired many social skills and has had corrective experiences that enable him to master situations and to appear superficially quite changed from the uncertain, awkward youngster he was. But is the change apparent or real? A closer look may reveal that he still makes successful use of the earlier compulsive defenses, but has tailored them to new, adult situations. He works with compulsive regularity and orderliness and experiences periodic increases in level of anxiety, as on weekends and vacations when he is unable to invest his energies in hard work; still, he has otherwise learned to live with his anxieties and to present the picture of a highly adequate individual. Thus, he has retained many of the early structures of his personality but utilizes them effectively in new ways in his present situation. Clearly, we could emphasize either the stability or the change in describing his personality, depending on our interest.

The significance of personality change is dealt with extensively by the phenomenologically oriented psychologist Carl Rogers, who maintains that human growth *requires* reorganization. For Rogers, psychotherapy is a matter of creating for the client conditions that make such reorganization, or growth, possible. On the basis of Rogers's concepts, the clinical psychologist Victor Raimy undertook a study of what happened to the self-concepts of clients during both successful and unsuccessful psychotherapy. The judgment of success was based on the opinions of clinical experts and supported by follow-up data on the clients after they left therapy. The graphs presented in Figure 4 illustrate his findings that, in cases considered successful, there

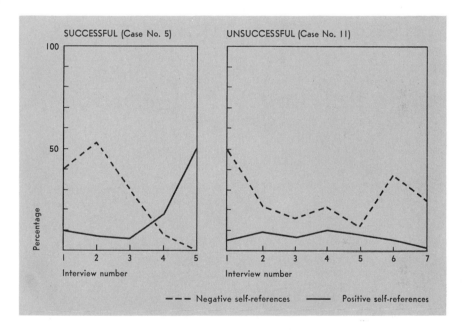

Figure 4. Changes in self-evaluation during psychotherapy. (Adapted from Raimy, V. C. Self-reference in counseling interviews. In Brayfield, A. H., ed., Modern methods of counseling. *New York: Appleton-Century-Crofts, 1950, Chapter 36, pp. 400–413. By permission,* J. Consul. Psychol.*)*

was an increase in positive self-references during the interviews and a decrease in negative self-references. In contrast, unsuccessful cases showed no such systematic improvement in self-evaluations. This study of Raimy's is a particularly well-known attempt to examine the principles of personality change; psychotherapy is clearly one of the best situations in which to make such observations.

It is crucial to theory construction that we understand not only the human capacity for reorganization but also the conditions that favor it. Besides, it is of practical importance because the possibilities of treatment or psychotherapy are linked to the capacity for personality change. We must know to what degree such change is possible for superficial characteristics as well as fundamental structures. Moreover, marked individual differences appear to exist in degree of stability or changeability of the personality. Unfortunately, psychologists interested in personality are in a very early stage of knowledge with respect to these problems, and we have little to go on since usable facts derived from research are in short supply.

Integration

Most developmentally oriented personologists visualize human development as a progression toward increasing structure, an integration of motivational, emotional, and cognitive parts. In the normal, healthy process of growth, a person advances from one level of organization to the next.

We have been considering consistency of personality as a matter of stable structures, but we can also regard it as more a matter of a mutually harmonious relationship among the structures. For the component parts must not, of course, be in conflict with one another, and what an individual does in one sphere of activity must accord with what he does in others or there is no consistency. Writers on this subject have sometimes regarded self-consistency as the ultimate goal of personality development. In this view, a person strives to harmonize every brush stroke in his picture of himself, so that all are put into perspective by some common principle or set of values. Similar conceptions of consistency are found in the writings of Carl Rogers, with his emphasis on maintaining and enhancing the self-concept, and of other phenomenologically oriented psychologists, such as Kurt Goldstein.

Goldstein, whose first interests were the structure and organization of the nervous system, has written about personality along lines parallel to his earlier neurological theories. For Goldstein, the *normal* organism is organized, or integrated, and disorganization—the isolation of function of the individual parts from the total system—is equivalent to pathology. Goldstein observed in persons with damaged cerebral cortices efforts to avoid the "catastrophic reaction," that is, the tension aroused when a neurologically defective individual is unable to come to terms with his environment effectively. A consequence of neurological damage, with its attendant disorganization and adaptive deficits, is the mounting of severe anxiety under conditions that the individual cannot master. Thus, for Goldstein, the normal, or healthy, state is characterized by harmonious interaction of the parts of the personality system, the pathological by lack of integration.

Just as pathology for Goldstein is synonymous with disorganization of the nervous system, so abnormality for the specialist in abnormal behavior is regression from higher levels of functioning and organization to developmentally earlier, or more primitive levels. Regression, therefore, is the opposite of integration, for it means the loss of the integration that is normally achieved in the course of progressive development. Although the terms and concepts developed for this state differ somewhat from writer to writer—including "dedifferentiation," "primitivization," "decompensation," and in the most general usage "regression"—one central idea is common to all: the breakdown of higher functions and levels of integration while the person struggles, often unsuccessfully, to meet demands or cope with stress. The term regression is used especially to describe what happens in that most severe psychological disorder, schizophrenia. A regressed patient can no longer function at the mature adult level. He behaves primitively, like a child, often being unable or unwilling to bathe, feed, or dress himself.

Consistency in the sense of harmonious integration implies that man does not act willy-nilly, the various parts of his personality independently going every which way, rather, personality is a coordinated system whose central structures direct activity in self-congruent ways. Normal or ideal development means growth and integration—that is, progression from lower, or primitive, stages to more advanced ones—whereas pathology or disorder means destruction of the advanced stages of integration and failure to sustain a fully integrated system.

So far, we have been talking about general qualities of personality, and it is now time to turn to some of the specific personality constructs that are typical of most theories of personality.

SPECIFIC CONSTRUCTS OF PERSONALITY

Although each theorist emphasizes somewhat different structures and processes, nearly all of them include two particular personality constructs in some form or other: motivation and control. Let us examine these in some detail. In our brief discussion here, we shall point up some aspects of motivation and control that are important to an understanding of their role in personality.

Motivation as a Personality Construct

The concept of motivation in psychology has a common-sense flavor because it easily fits into our phenomenal experience and language. Man had motivational concepts long before psychology came into being as a systematic discipline. We talk about wanting or desiring something, wishing, intending, and so on. We think of our actions as motivated, that is, as deliberate efforts to obtain what we want, therefore as "caused" by motivation.

Motivation implies *direction*—goals toward which our behavior is oriented. We wish, for example, to get a job rather than be idle and without income, to eat rather than go hungry, and to be liked instead of disliked. In addition to direction, motivation encompasses the quality of *intensity*. We commonly speak of strong or weak motives; we observe a person expending great effort and displaying dogged persistence in some activities, while in others he gives evidence of limited desire; we want some things very much and others scarcely at all.

Motive is the hypothetical construct denoting certain forces that impel behavior. Every theory of personality makes use of some version of the concept of motive, even though the precise details vary. Diverse terms such as motive, drive, need, impulse, id, wish, want, or valence indicate these con-

Fundamental
Qualities
and Structures
of Personality

ceptual differences. But in spite of variation in precise meaning, the large concept is common—the idea that some identifiable force activates and directs behavior. This force is preceded by certain specifiable conditions and produces certain given effects in behavior.

Knowing that personality itself is an inference, we can immediately recognize that the specific personality construct of motivation is theoretical, too. We cannot witness a person's wishes, needs, or urges. But we can watch what he does and says and some of the conditions surrounding his actions. These empirically observable events permit us to infer his motivation.

The great bulk of research on motives has to do with the conditions that activate them. A laboratory experimenter, for example, motivates his subjects by issuing instructions or by manipulating incentives (reward and punishment). For a personality psychologist, however, motivation is not only a transient state produced by external conditions, but an intrinsic characteristic of a person, a characteristic that, so to speak, he carries about with him from time to time and circumstance to circumstance. If the component parts of personality are consistent, then the kind or pattern of motives in a person, their strength, and the likelihood of their being aroused in any given situation constitute a stable quality of personality. To speak of some individuals as ambitious and of others as security-minded is to describe them in terms of motivational characteristics. In fact, the full description of personality usually includes the assessment of intrinsic motives.

To make an adequate description of personality in terms of motivation, obviously, we must have some classification of motives. Moreover, the motives in our list must have behavioral referents, that is we must identify the empirical observations that permit us to infer whether one or another motive is present or to distinguish between the strengths of two motivations. An example of such a classification is that of the well-known psychologist Henry Murray. He uses the term *need* to stand for a psychological force that organizes action and perception and other cognitive processes toward its own satisfaction. Murray following tradition, classifies needs into primary, or viscerogenic, and secondary, or psychogenic. In Table 2, we list some of those primary and secondary needs that Murray regards as important, along with short descriptions of each.

Murray's system is only one of the many that are possible. For psychologists debate vigorously about proper and useful classification. One point of controversy is whether some needs should be added or deleted from the list; another is the origin of needs. Moreover, to describe personality in terms of the most important needs that characterize it requires more than merely listing them. Differences in motivation among people are likely to be less a matter of having or not having certain needs than of how they are organized, of their relative importance for each person. Thus, in one person, achievement needs may predominate, whereas in another affiliation needs may be the most powerful. This is not to say that the man driven primarily by striving for achievement is not interested in affiliation; rather, that the former is more powerful in energizing and directing his behavior. Knowing this, we can predict that, when he is given a choice of action, to the degree that achievement needs predominate, he will take directions in his behavior that offer opportunities to compete successfully against some standard of excellence. In contrast, if affiliation needs predominate he will strive mainly to establish warm, friendly, personal relations with others. It is necessary, therefore, to describe need systems within an individual as organized hierarchies, that is, in terms of their relative importance in determining behavior. As we shall see in Chapter 5, different theories of personality stress different needs or motives, but all make use of the concept of motivation in some form.

TABLE 2

Important Examples of Primary and Secondary Needs

Primary

A. Lacks $\begin{cases} \text{Water} \\ \text{Food} \end{cases}$

B. Distentions $\begin{cases} \text{Secretions} \begin{cases} \text{Sex} \\ \text{Lactation} \end{cases} \\ \text{Excretions} \begin{cases} \text{Urination} \\ \text{Defecation} \end{cases} \end{cases}$

C. Harms $\begin{cases} \text{Heat Avoidance} \\ \text{Cold Avoidance} \end{cases}$

Secondary

Acquisition—need to gain possessions and property.
Achievement—need to overcome obstacles, exercise power and try to do a difficult task well and quickly.
Dominance—need to influence or control others.
Autonomy—need to resist influence or coercion.
Aggression—need to assault or harm another.
Affiliation—need to form friendships and associations.
Nurturance—need to nourish, aid, or protect helpless people.
Succorance—need to seek help, protection, or sympathy.
Cognizance—need to inquire, explore, seek knowledge, and satisfy curiosity.

From Murray, H. A., *Explorations in personality.* New York: Oxford University Press, 1938.

Now, although motivation is a central construct of personality, by itself it is insufficient to explain individual differences in personality. For one thing, it is apparent that in normal transactions with the social and physical environment we are constrained from expressing some motives although we are permitted to discharge others freely. With the exception of small children and exceedingly immature adults, when we feel anger we do not necessarily express it toward others through destructive aggression. The expression of anger, then, is inhibited, especially when aggression is likely to be punished by some form of retaliation or when a person regards it as wrong or improper. Similarly, the arousal of sexual feelings does not necessarily lead to immediate and indiscriminate sexual play. Since many motives within us simultaneously compete for expression, lest our behavior be chaotic we must follow one direction at the expense of many others. The point is that room must be made in any system of personality theory for inhibition of, or control over, the expression of motives, for it is control that permits a person to program his behavior, to determine which motive to express and which to suppress.

Fundamental
Qualities
and Structures
of Personality

Control as a Personality Construct

As with motivation, psychologists have proposed many alternative concepts for the executive role in the personality and have developed many names for them. Freud, for one, employed the word ego to refer to the control mechanisms of the personality. And others have used terms such as regulation, inhibition, style, self, ego-defense, and ego-control to represent the structures of control. Such professional usage is somewhat analogous to the lay idea of self-control, for that term, too, represents in a general way the capacity of an individual to inhibit the expression of undesirable impulses in favor of considerations of safety, conscience, or future welfare. Most personality theories, then, have these two common elements: the concept of motivation to cover what excites action and impels it toward some goal and the concept of control to cover selective inhibition of impulses.

Besides the function of simply *inhibiting* impulses, in some theories the concept of control covers another function, namely, transforming them so that a motive originally directed toward one goal is expressed in another, usually more acceptable way. This notion of transformation probably originated with Freud's concept of sublimation. Freud maintained that the creative and esthetic features of our complex modern society really derive from sublimated, or transformed, sexual and aggressive energies that are denied direct expression by social taboos. By transformation, though, man can partially express primitive sexual urges in the creation, or appreciation, of beautiful music or other art forms. Earlier we discussed some ways that society permits the safe and approved discharge of aggression, as in spectator or competitive sports. In Freud's thinking, the healthy person is someone whose ego is effective enough to permit the greatest discharge of these primitive urges in a manner that is socially acceptable. Failure results in the flooding of the personality by stimulation from anxiety-producing impulses and the consequent development of pathological symptoms. Since Freud, many personality theorists have tended to regard the adequacy of control mechanisms (sometimes referred to as ego-strength) as crucial to the task of finding satisfactory routes for gratifying motives and functioning in a healthy fashion.

Actually, we know relatively little about the control characteristics of normal, or effective, persons, or about the conditions that determine the development of the control processes. Recently, personality researchers have attempted to study degree of control as an important criterion for describing personality. Psychologist Jack Block has developed a test by which people can be characterized as normal controllers, undercontrollers (insufficiently capable of inhibiting impulses), or overcontrollers (too severely inhibited in expressing their needs). Some examples of test items suggesting overcontrol and undercontrol may be found in Table 3. And other researchers have become increasingly interested in what the control mechanisms of personality are and how they can be identified by observing behavior in various situations.

One form of control that has usually been identified with psychopathology is the ego-defense mechanism, a topic we discussed briefly in our previous treatment of psychopathology.

TABLE 3

Questions from the Block Personality Test of Control

Overcontrol Items	*Scored Response*
2. I am very slow in making up my mind.	True
7. I usually feel nervous and ill at ease at a formal dance or party.	True
11. When in a group of people, I have trouble thinking of the right things to talk about.	True
14. When I work on a Committee, I like to take charge of things.	False
17. I like to talk before groups of people.	False
18. I am a good mixer.	False

Undercontrol Items	
2. I am often said to be hotheaded.	True
5. I would disapprove of anyone's drinking to the point of intoxication at a party.	False
11. I often act on the spur of the moment without stopping to think.	True
15. I like to plan a home study schedule and then follow it.	False
20. I find it easy to "drop" or "break with" a friend.	True
22. I never make judgments about people until I am sure of the facts.	False

From Block, J., Neurotic overcontrol and undercontrol items in the California Personality Inventory as developed by H. Gough.

HOW IS PERSONALITY DEFINED?

We have described personality as an organization of relatively stable hypothetical structures by virtue of which a person acts in a particular way and which must be inferred from behavior. And while we have illustrated this point with two general examples, motivation and control, we have not fully described personality. We have indicated the most important formal qualities of personality, but not its content. How then can we specify the constructs of personality more definitely and indicate the rules of their organization? The influential theorist Gordon Allport approached the problem by defining personality as *"the dynamic organization within the individual of those psychophysical systems that determine his unique adjustments to his environment."* This is a good definition. But what are these psychophysical systems (the constructs of personality)? What is their dynamic organization? How can we describe a person's unique adjustments to his environment? We have, in a sense, already defined personality in a way similar to Allport, as an organization of stable structures within a person that dispose him to act in certain ways.

Actually, we have gone as far as we can toward the definition of personality without adopting some particular theory of personality. For example, Freud introduced one particular set of constructs in building his theoretical model of personality. This model included a special terminology for constructs and a special set of laws for their organization. Similarly, Kurt Lewin developed his own distinctive conceptual system. Psychologists of other persuasions

Fundamental
Qualities
and Structures
of Personality

have also ventured into the realm of personality-theory construction to a greater or lesser degree, each yielding different specific postulates about the structures and processes of personality.

In a presentation such as this, though, we feel it is best not to accept any special system. Instead, we prefer to provide the reader with information that will help him understand the chief issues in the science of personality. Further, we should like to suggest as broadly as we can how the different systems diverge and converge in handling these issues. In Chapter 5 we shall attempt to present an overview of personality theories without going into detail or committing ourselves on any one. Although our presentation should help clarify questions about the substance of personality as various theorists envision it, there is no substitute for reading in the actual primary sources.

Personality Theory

It is often distressing to the beginning student to discover how many diverse ways there are of conceptualizing personality. The myriad of theoretical systems is so confusing that he is frustrated in his desire to have simple, authoritative statements about the structure and dynamics of personality. This multiplicity of theories reflects two things—first, the great richness and complexity of personality, and second, the early stage the science of personality is still in.

The science of personality as a self-conscious discipline is a very new one, having got under way shortly before the turn of the century. Yet learned men have speculated

5

about such matters for thousands of years, and their ideas make up part of the philosophical background for modern theoretical systems. Among the speculators were the Greek philosophers Aristotle and Plato and the great Greek physician Hippocrates; the latter introduced a long-lasting personality typology based on the now-discarded idea that temperament depends on the distribution in the body of certain fluids (see p. 56).

The simultaneous presence today of many systematic and viable treatments of personality tells us that the science of personality is still at a somewhat early stage of development. If we knew enough and had a sufficiently comprehensive conceptual framework, those theories that were less adequate would be discarded. And even though scientific theories are always being revised or replaced, the presence of so many side by side suggests inadequacies in their present formulation and in the available evidence with which to evaluate them. Yet they remain active because, in spite of many similarities among them, each contributes something that the others do not. The great challenge to the personality theorist and researcher is to advance us beyond our present limits with respect to both conceptualizations and relevant empirical data.

At the present time, neither the student nor the expert can know the field of personality unless he is also aware of the variety of theoretical systems designed to encompass it. As a start in this direction, in this chapter we shall analyze a number of issues by which the theories themselves can be compared, rather than attempt in so small a space to describe any theory in detail. To supplement this skeletal account it is important for the reader to turn to more elaborate primary or secondary sources. He may read the fascinating material written by the great names in personality theory—Freud, Sullivan, Allport, Lewin, Rogers, to mention a few—or he may avail himself of one of several excellent recent secondary treatments cited at the end of the book. It is hoped that the overview presented here will provide an intellectual framework in which to place the often bewildering array of ideas about personality.

Each personality theory differs from the others in some of its tenets about the nature of the person. These differences have become intensely debated issues, and the theories can be compared by their resolutions of each of the issues. Sometimes two theories will be similar in their handling of one issue but extremely unlike in approaching another. The remainder of this chapter will be devoted to a consideration of each of the main issues and a comparison of how the principal theories of personality deal with them. The issues include: (1) frame of reference, (2) the nature of human motivation, and (3) the postulated, or assumed, interplay of personality, culture, and inherited physical constitution. We shall often cite influential theoretical systems to illustrate our points, but our treament requires that we ignore some and emphasize others to avoid confusion. Let us first proceed to examine the theoretical frames of reference of personality theories.

THEORETICAL FRAMES OF REFERENCE

We must first consider the nature of a psychological event in order to identify some of the frames of reference in which it may be regarded. There are three components of any psychological event. The first is the *stimulus* to which a person responds. The last is his *response*. The other component is made up of the states and activities in the *organism* in between the first and last. We cannot directly observe these states and activities, which are sometimes called mediating structures and processes, but we assume that they intervene between stimulus and response. We have already seen examples of them in the form of motivation and control.

The exact definition of stimulus is a source of controversy. Some hold that we can identify a stimulus only by physical measurements, such as wave lengths of light or decibels of sound. Others hold that we must define a stimulus by the reactions it induces, such as the interpretations a person gives some physical object. The meaning of response is broad: It can include not only obvious actions like reaching for something, but also, what is more difficult to identify, the styles of action. We may include as a response even the internal physiological accompaniments of a psychological event, such as the changes in heart activity or respiration that are associated with emotional states such as fear or anger. Still, in spite of the ambiguity of these terms, psychologists in analyzing psychological events have found it useful to think in terms of stimulus, the intervening structures and processes of the organism, and response.

The S-O-R analysis also turns out to be an excellent way of distinguishing among different frames of reference in personality theory. A frame of reference in itself is not precisely a theory, rather it is the philosophic basis of a theory because it delineates assumptions and emphases. Some theorists, for instance, tend to focus on responses, others on the intervening processes (such as subjective interpretations of stimuli), and still others on the physical qualities of stimuli. Although these variations in assumption and emphasis are not, as we shall see, the only sources of disagreement among persons with differing theoretical orientations, they are fundamental and important. Sometimes, however, several specific theories can be grouped together because they agree in their basic S-O-R frame of reference.

Now we shall examine three frames of reference that diverge with respect to stimulus, organism, and response. The first, trait-and-type, falls on the response side of the S-O-R analysis; the second, the stimulus-response-associative-learning frame of reference, centers around physical stimuli and how habits of response are acquired; finally, the phenomenological approach, which defines the stimulus subjectively—that is, how a person apprehends it— focuses mainly on the intervening structures and processes. All current personality theories may in fact, be subsumed under these three basic frames of reference. Although a given theory may incorporate more than one frame of reference, any theory or part of a theory can be analyzed along these lines.

The Trait-and-Type Frame of Reference

The simplest and most traditional way of describing a person's personality is to identify his consistent patterns of behavior and label them with trait names. Every language contains large numbers of words that define traits of personality. We describe people as shy, aggressive, submissive, lazy, melancholy, easy-going, ambitious, and so on. But what do we mean when we use such terms? And how can this common sense approach to the description of personality become a systematic scientific enterprise?

The Trait Approach.   If we observe a person in a variety of situations and note that he always allows someone else to take the initiative in deciding what to do, we have reason to think that this tendency is a consistent part of his personality. We have only to interpret it and to find a term that describes it—say, "submissiveness." If such a descriptive term applies to a person in a wide variety of situations, then we can fairly claim it as a trait. The more consistent the behavior and the more frequent its occurrence in dissimilar situations, the more clearly and importantly characteristic the trait. In the trait approach to personality, then, we identify the most important characteristics in human personality and analyze their organization.

We said earlier that the trait approach is largely oriented to response characteristics. Let us consider how this is so. We know that we identify traits by observing a person behave consistently in response to a variety of stimuli. Thus, to identify a trait we must observe characteristic responses occurring independently of the stimulus context (pattern of stimuli to which the person is exposed). For it is just those responses that are not governed by the stimulus context and therefore recur in a variety of circumstances that define a trait. The trait approach to personality requires, then, that stimuli be held constant or ruled out and that a person's responses be clearly attributes or dispositions that belong to him rather than the situation. To the degree that a trait theorist is interested in forces within personality that determine consistent patterns of behavior, he introduces intervening structures and processes into his system.

The model of the trait approach to personality is the *psychogram*. The psychogram is a schematization of a person's several traits whereby he is described by how much he has of certain traits as compared with other persons. Thus, using a given group as the standard, or norm, we say he has a lot of one trait, less of another, and very little of a third. We can express his resulting pattern in a graph or chart, and so for anyone else. A modern personality assessment tool recently developed by Harrison Gough at the University of California is the California Personality Inventory. It makes use of psychograms or profiles of personality based on the scores obtained from answers a person gives to questions in a series of subtests, each measuring

Figure 5. An example of a psychogram, or personality profile, based on scores on the California Personality Inventory. Male, age 18. This profile is marked by a general elevation of those scales having to do with poise, ascendancy, and self-assurance, and a general lowering of those indicative of socialization, maturity, and sense of responsibility. These trends are highlighted by the elevation on the self-acceptance scale and the low point on the measure of socialization. From an examination of the profile, a picture of this boy can be evolved. Our expectation is that he would be assertive, socially forward, probably self-centered and overbearing, rebellious, impulsive, undependable, and overconcerned with personal gain and pleasure. Because of his very considerable social skills he might function adequately, in the sense of attaining his own ends and objectives; yet, his deficiencies in the area of responsibility and interpersonal maturity seem almost certainly to destine him for social friction and difficulty. (Note: This boy was one of the three in his class of over 400 high school students who was identified by the principal as a "serious disciplinary problem.") (From Gough, H. G. California Psychological Inventory Manual. Palo Alto, California: Consulting Psychologists Press, Inc., 1957.)

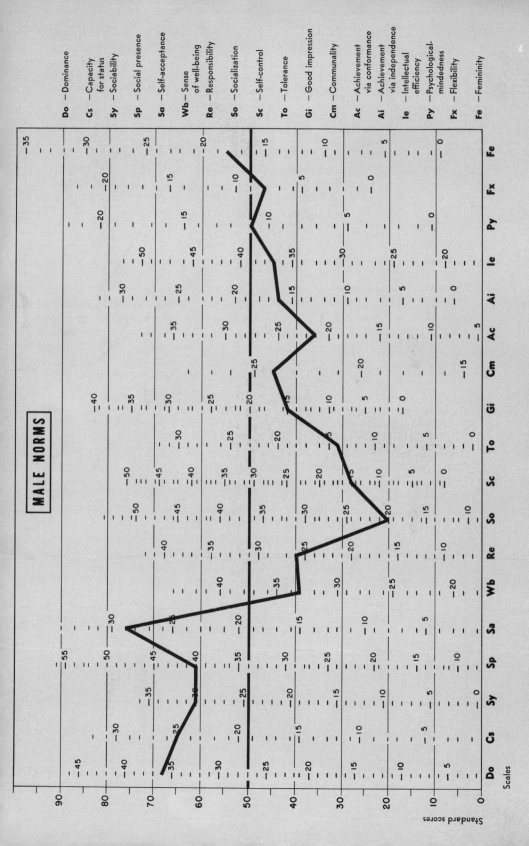

different traits. Figure 5 shows a high school student's test profile based on this test; a brief personality description of the student appears in the legend (p. 54). The whole question of personality assessment will be taken up in more detail in Chapter 7. Here we wish merely to illustrate the psychogram as the model of a trait approach to personality.

The Type Approach.   Personality typologies are built on a response-oriented frame of reference that is very similar to that involved in traits. The difference is that whereas in the latter approach we assign a variety of traits to a person, as in a psychogram, in the type approach we adopt a much broader, unifying scheme of classification, or pigeonholing. The type approach, then, is an extension of the trait approach. By the pattern of his traits we can classify a person. If he shares a trait pattern with a large group of other individuals, we can simplify the description: Instead of listing each trait according to the extent he has it, we use a few categories for characteristic patterns. Thus, we observe that shyness tends to go with other qualities, such as an inclination to be introspective, easily hurt, and so on, and we can identify this grouping of traits by a single inclusive category called introversion. And we can identify a complementary type called extroversion. Having isolated these two categories, we can say that because such-and-such a person has such-and-such traits he is a member of one or the other type.

Just as the vocabulary of traits has existed for thousands of years, so have typologies. The best known typology in ancient Greece was that of Hippocrates, in the fifth century B.C. Conceiving that the body contained four fluids, or humors—yellow bile, black bile, phlegm, and blood—Hippocrates speculated that personality depended on which of these humors predominated in a person's constitution. Thus, yellow bile went with a choleric or irascible temperament, black bile with melancholy, phlegm with the sluggish, apathetic, or phlegmatic person, and blood with the cheerful, active, sanguine personality.

Among the best-known modern typologies of personality is that of Carl Jung, an early associate of Freud. Jung's typology includes two broad categories—the *extrovert,* who is oriented primarily toward others and the external world, and the *introvert,* who is more preoccupied with himself and his subjective world. Extroversion and introversion are expressed in a variety of functions, including thinking, feeling, sensing, and intuiting, so that, in actuality, Jung's typology is more complex than people usually realize. For example, one could be a thinking extrovert, but an introvert in the intuitive function. Another familiar personality typology is that of Freud himself, who conceived of types according to his theory of psychosexual development. In this theory Freud proposed that everyone passes through three infantile psychosexual stages distinguished according to the primary means of sexual gratification. In the oral stage erotic activity centers around the lips and mouth, in the anal stage on bowel activity and the stimulation of the mucous membranes of the anus, and in the phallic stage on the genital organs.

In the course of development some individuals, because of traumatic experiences at one or another stage, fail to progress normally to the next stage. When they are adults, the primitive psychosexual tendencies characteristic of the respective immature stages continue to remain active, governing their personalities and producing characteristic psychological traits. Thus, Freud identified three types: oral, anal, and phallic. The *oral type* is characterized by dependent attitudes toward others. He continues to seek sustenance, or feeding, from others, and, depending on when during the oral stage fixation occurred, is either optimistic, immature, and trusting, or pessimistic, suspicious, and sarcastic, about the prospects of continuing support. The *anal type* is also characterized by two substages, the first identified by outbursts of aggression, sloppiness, and petulance, the second associated with obstinacy, orderliness, and parsimoniousness. The *phallic type* is characterized by an adolescent immaturity in which the predominant conflicts are heterosexual, stemming from the Oedipus complex and the anxieties associated with it. The phallic period is stormy, with sharp emotional swings and preoccupation with love object choices. Adults with severe disturbances in childhood development can be classified into oral, anal, and phallic types according to when the psychosexual disturbance occurred and what types of behavior pattern they display as a result.

There are many other personality typologies. Usually, as with those of Jung and Freud, rather than being merely simple, independent classification schemes of behavior, they are also based on theoretical propositions about the structure, dynamics, and development of personality. The reader should consult the other sources listed at the end of the volume for elaboration of these systems.

From a practical standpoint, the trait-and-type approach is most useful when the pertinent behavior patterns are absolutely consistent—that is, characteristic of a person regardless of circumstances. What limits the usefulness of any trait or type system is the problem of degree of trait generality. The statement that a person has the trait of submissiveness is useful for prediction only insofar as he is submissive in all or most situations. If he is submissive only in certain circumstances, then we can predict his behavior accurately only if we know what those circumstances are.

This puts the finger on the most serious deficiency of the trait-and-type approach to personality, namely, that it largely ignores the dynamic interchange between a person and his environment. For the stimulus context normally limits the manifestations of trait characteristics.

The problem of prediction also suggests the weakness of typologies: They are likely to be so excessively broad that a classification will apply to a person only to a limited degree except in extreme instances. Identifying someone as anal, for example, is useful so long as it permits us to expect such characteristic behavior as obstinacy or orderliness. But few people are so inordinately typical that they are obstinate or orderly in every situation that may arise.

Thus, the trait-and-type approach is limited by focusing exclusively on responses and assuming that personality structures are static properties that can be inferred from consistencies of response, rather than adaptive transactions with the environment. Because of this critical limitation, psychologists have constructed other frames of reference that pay more attention to the stimulus context. Let us now turn to one of these, the stimulus-response-associative-learning approach, and examine how it handles this difficulty in the trait-and-type frame of reference.

Stimulus-Response-Associative-Learning Theory (SRAL)

The central concern of SRAL theorists is the problem of how organisms acquire habits of response. They have traditionally attempted to discover the details of the learning process, to find out how connections are established between stimuli and responses in juxtaposition (association) so that when a given stimulus, or one similar to it, recurs, it will induce the same, or similar, response. In their theories of learning they try to specify *how* these connections are made, strengthened, or broken.

Besides elevating the question of how habits or traits are acquired, the SRAL frame of reference stands on the physical stimulus side of the S-O-R sequence. Instead of being built around correlations among responses as the trait-and-type frame of reference is, associative-learning approaches rest on correlations between physical stimuli and responses.

Although SRAL theorists were originally concerned entirely with principles of learning, some came to recognize that their propositions might have general application to other fields, such as personality. Personality psychologists have, in fact, tended simply to accept the learning process as given, without much concern about its details, even though they usually assume that personality structure develops, in part, through learning. To fill the gap, therefore, learning theoreticians with broad concerns such as Edwin Guthrie in past years and John Dollard and Neal Miller in recent years have attempted to carry associative-learning theory into the realm of personality. But exactly how does personality become established through the learning process?

Dollard and Miller identify four concepts of prime importance in the learning process—drive, response, cue, and reinforcement. *Drive* is what initiates responses. It originates as tissue needs, which, when unsatisfied, produce internal discomforts that lead a person to activities that may or may not satisfy it. *Reinforcement* of a drive is the product of responses that do satisfy the need. Thus, if the need for food produces drive, the response of eating reinforces the hunger drive by fulfilling it and so terminates that behavior sequence. Learning, then, is the establishment of *responses* that reinforce under conditions of drive—that is, responses which reduce or eliminate the drive. Learning also requires the establishment of connections between such responses and certain *cues,* or stimuli, in the environment. Thus, if the reinforcing response is eating, a person must identify those stimuli to which the response is appropriate. These situations may involve the presence of food or environmental circumstances under which food may be found—for instance, a refrigerator can be an appropriate cue for obtaining food. In sum, under conditions of drive, and in the presence of cues, or stimuli, a person makes responses that reinforce the drive, and those responses that do are learned in association with those cues.

In addition to these fundamental factors, Dollard and Miller identify certain other characteristics of learning. The strengthening of connections between certain cues and drive-reinforcing responses implies the converse weakening of other connections and the elimination of inappropriate responses that may have been tried before. This elimination of previously learned responses is called *extinction.* This process is essential to learning, for learning could not take place unless, along with the establishment and strengthening of desired responses, unwanted acts were extinguished.

According to still another principle of SRAL theory, *stimulus generalization,* responses that have been learned in association with one specific cue may be transferred to other similar situations. If we have learned to be afraid of speaking up in one particular social situation, the response of fear is likely to be induced by other social situations as well. The greater the similarity between stimuli, the more the likelihood that a response that has been learned to one stimulus will generalize to the other; and conversely, the less the similarity, the less the likelihood. Since no two situations are ever precisely the same, consistency of behavior would never occur without stimulus generalization. The perception of stimulus similarity, it is generally thought, is based on the physical features of the stimuli. But actually specifying which physical quality is critical remains one of the most perplexing unsolved problems in learning theory, since we can respond similarly to stimuli on the basis of many physical dimensions. The cues of similarity to which a person responds or fails to respond are difficult, if not impossible, to predict without a knowledge of intervening structures and processes.

If responses learned to one stimulus tended to generalize indiscriminately to others, learning could not occur, since the same response could then be made to all. For adaptive behavior to develop, a person must learn to distinguish among stimuli so that he makes reinforcing responses to the correct one. To give a concrete example, he must learn to differentiate a refrigerator that contains food from a cabinet that contains material incapable of reducing his hunger drive. The process by which we differentiate appropriate from inappropriate cues is called *discrimination.* Just as stimulus generalization is required in order for a person to spread a given response to all members of a class of appropriate cues, so discrimination is required to permit him to select the proper class of cues that will produce drive reduction.

Finally, through *anticipation,* another process postulated by associative-learning theory, we identify the probable consequences of a stimulus or response; thereby we can learn to perform actions that will reduce a drive in the future and to avoid those that will have painful or dangerous consequences. Anticipation, which involves making a response earlier than it would normally occur, helps the individual react appropriately to an impending situation about which he has been alerted.

According to SRAL theory, complex social motives, such as the desire to achieve or to be liked, are learned in the same way as any other simpler type of response, such as tying a shoe or hitting a typewriter key. Rewards can also be learned. Thus, we learn to accept expressions of approval as rewards because the approval has become associated in childhood with the reinforcement, by parents or other adults, of primary drives like hunger and thirst. In other words, we have learned that approval is connected with desirable consequences even though social approval itself originally had no intrinsic value.

According to the principles of learning briefly sketched above, it is plain that we can learn complex patterns of response, including neurotic symptoms, such as phobias and hysterical paralyses characteristic of certain types of neurotic disorder as well as the defense mechanisms connected with these disorders. Defense mechanisms as responses—although they are maladjustments in the sense that, in using them, we distort reality in our perceptions and judgments—do reduce the drives of anxiety and fear. Clearly, then, any characteristic of personality—motives, control processes, defense mechanisms, and so on—is learned according to the same set of laws specified by learning theorists.

For *our* analysis of frames of reference, the important feature of SRAL theory is its emphasis on the physical stimulus. The point is that from this position the stimulus to a behavioral act can be defined in terms of physical dimensions (such as wave lengths, shape, weight, size, and distance) and completely independently of the person behaving—that is, responding. And since it is these objective characteristics to which the person presumably responds, we can construct behavioral laws by separately identifying the physical characteristics of environmental stimuli and the characteristics of responses made in association with these stimuli. The basic unit of description is the stimulus-response connection.

It is a direct attack on this emphasis on the physical stimulus that identifies the phenomenological point of view, the third major frame of reference in personality theory.

Personality from a Phenomenological Point of View

For a theorist in the phenomenological camp, defining a stimulus physically immediately poses a problem, namely, that our perception of objects is not necessarily identical with the objects themselves. Our senses do not directly transmit physical objects. Rather, we respond to representations of objects—that is, objects as mediated by our perceptual apparatuses and by our individual interpretations. In an effort to articulate the distinction, psychologists interested in perception have termed the physical object itself the "distal stimulus," and the object as mediated by intervening mechanisms the "proximal stimulus." The phenomenologist argues that what determine responses are not physical objects themselves but the intervening structures and processes within a person that mediate the physical stimuli. He reconstructs the causes of action through inferences about these psychological representations of external stimuli. Thus, in phenomenological approaches to personality the stimulus in the S-O-R analysis is still significant, but as a psychological representation within a person, not as an external physical condition. Here the emphasis is on the O, and the psychological representation of a physical stimulus may deviate sharply from physical reality.

The essence of the phenomenological frame of reference to personality is this: The cause of action is the world as a person apprehends it privately. This privately apprehended world is the core construct of the theoretical systems of such phenomenologists as Kurt Lewin and Carl Rogers. In Lewin's system the term employed for the construct is *life space,* in Rogers' it is *phenomenal field.*

For Lewin the psychological representation of the world (the life space) consists of the person's needs and the potentialities of action available, as he apprehends them. Every aspect of a person's physical environment that is not part of the life space and to which he does not directly respond is the "foreign hull" of the life space. To understand his behavior at any point in time we must reconstruct and describe the life space, which means that we must understand the psychological forces in operation at that moment.

These forces are described by a Lewinian graphically in diagrams that include: goal regions (shown as enclosed places); positive and negative valences (designated by plus or minus signs), which identify desirable or undesirable aspects of the life space; vectors (arrows), which point out the directions to which a person is pulled; and barriers (lines separating the person from positive goals), which block or slow down a person's approach to any goal region. Many forces may affect the person, and his behavior at any time is a resultant of them. Not only can the total psychological field (called the life space) be thus represented diagrammatically, but the structure of the individual personality can also be diagrammed topologically as was illustrated earlier in Figure 3. An example of a Lewinian diagram of the life space and its interpretation is presented in Figure 6.

The important elements in the Lewinian system are these: Psychological events are considered in terms of the construct of life space, which comprises subjective definitions of the environment, and some of the psychodynamic laws that pertain to it are identified diagrammatically. The system makes use of both motivational and cognitive structures in continual interplay. Inferences about a person's life space are always derived from systematic observation of his behavior in his environment. Yet the terms of the analysis of behavior and setting are not static traits and stationary objects but the person's own subjective apprehension of his environment and his relationship to it.

In contrast with Lewin's brand of phenomenology is the self theory of Rogers, whose concepts are also couched in the language of subjective experience (for example, what we want and how we think and feel). The Rogerian concept that is analogous to life space is phenomenal field, and the core (or most important aspect) of that field is the *self-concept* of the individual, that is, his notion of who he is in relation to his environment. It is this self-concept that determines his behavior. This phenomenal self is, for a person himself, reality. He does not respond to the objective environment but to what he perceives it to be, regardless of how distorted or personalized his perception may be. These subjective realities are tentative hypotheses that a person entertains about environmental situations.

Thus, one person will conceive of himself as a reformer with the mission of correcting certain worldly ills and helping others to "see the light." Another will view himself as a "realist," able to accept gracefully, and even benefit from, the weaknesses of human nature and man's social institutions. Self-concepts are complex and variable and they determine how persons will react to and deal with a wide variety of situations. These conceptions of who and what one is not only comprise central values and belief systems, but also include images of oneself as physically strong or weak, attractive or unattractive, popular or unpopular, and so on, based partly on the reflected appraisals of other people with whom one has had contact. According to self theorists, this differentiated portion of the phenomenal field, the self-concept,

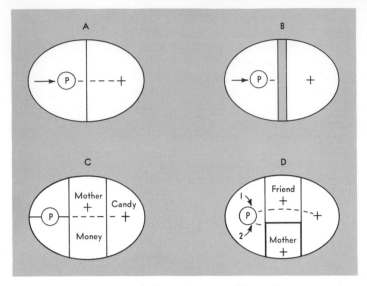

Figure 6. Lewinian diagram representing the changing life space of a child in a specific psychological transaction with his environment.

". . . a child passes a candy store, looks in the window, and wishes he had some candy. The sight of the candy arouses a need, and this need does three things. It releases energy and thereby arouses tension in an inner-personal region (the candy-wanting system). It confers a positive valence upon the region in which the candy is located. It creates a force which pushes the child in the direction of the candy.

"Let us say that the child has to enter the store and buy the candy. This situation can be represented by Figure A. Suppose, however, that the child does not have any money; then the boundary between him and the candy will be an impassable barrier. He will move as close to the candy as possible, perhaps putting his nose against the window, without being able to reach it (Figure B).

"He may say to himself, 'If I had some money, I could buy some candy. Maybe mother will give me some money.' In other words, a new need or quasi need, the intention to get some money from his mother, is created. This intention, in turn, arouses a tension, a vector, and a valence which are represented in Figure C. A thin boundary has been drawn between the child and the mother on the assumption that he has to go home, find his mother, and ask her for money. Another thin boundary has been drawn between the mother and the candy to represent the effort required to return to the store and make a purchase. The child moves to the candy by way of the mother.

"If the mother refuses to give the child any money, he may think of borrowing it from a friend. In this case, the region containing the mother is surrounded by an impenetrable barrier, and a new path through the region containing the friend to the candy is transcribed (Figure D).

"This topological representation could be endlessly complicated by introducing additional environmental regions and boundaries of varying degrees of firmness, and additional needs with their coordinated tension systems, valences, and vectors." (From Hall, C. S.; and Lindzey, G. Theories of personality. New York: Wiley, 1957, pp. 230–231.)

determines all behavior. And most behavior, indeed, is organized around efforts to preserve and enhance this phenomenal self.

While Lewin goes about the task of reconstructing a person's life space, with its multiplicity of psychological forces, from observing how he acts in different situations, Rogers identifies the self-concept largely from introspection. That is, a Rogerian learns about someone's self-system by listening to his introspective report about himself and his perceptions of the world. Lewin systematically observed behavior in various naturalistic and experimental situations, but Rogers developed his theoretical constructions primarily from psychotherapy. He argued that to the degree that he could provide an environment of permissiveness and support, a patient's reports would validly reflect his whole phenomenal field and his narrower self-concept.

Regardless of the exact form of the phenomenological system, however, it is clear that it shifts theoretical attention from the physical stimulus itself to the way a person apprehends it and, therefore, to the properties of the person that mediate between the physical stimulus and behavior. Thus, to recapitulate, although trait-and-type theory is response-centered and associative-learning theory is stimulus-response-centered, phenomenological theory revolves around the properties of the person that intervene between the stimulus and the behavioral response.

All theories of personality are variations of one sort or another of the three main frames of reference derived from the stimulus, organism, and response sequence. Some theories, as we have seen, are in the main anchored to one or another of these three points of view. Other systems, such as that of Freud, are mixtures, in that they draw on features of all three frames of reference. For example, psychoanalysis contains features of the trait-and-type approach, yet its essential character does not fall in that category. The point to remember is that the frames of reference described do not specify individual theoretical systems, but rather orientations or emphases that vary among them.

We are now prepared to proceed to the second principal issue on which theoretical systems diverge—the nature of motivation.

THE NATURE OF HUMAN MOTIVATION

Every theory of personality must deal with the problem of human motivation. Stripped of its nonessentials the problem is twofold: What are the fundamental human motives and how did they originate?

The Tension-Reduction Model

Associative-learning theory
as applied to personality and as represented by Dollard and Miller divides all human motivation into two general categories, primary drives and secondary drives. As for the so-called *primary drives,* man is assumed to be born with certain tissue needs that must be satisfied to permit survival and freedom from tension or pain. We must, for example, take nourishment, replenish water, get sleep, and sustain a limited variation in body temperature. These needs are present in us as part of our inherent physiological construction and require no learning. Primary drives arise directly from these tissue needs. We learn the behavior that enables us to gratify those needs and reduce their related drive.

Secondary, or derived, drives do not arise from the inherent tissue needs. Rather, they are learned through social experiences. We learn such drives because we connect certain behaviors associated with them to the reduction or satisfaction of primary drives. For example, a young child links the affectional responses of his mother in feeding him with the elimination of, say, hunger. Therefore, he learns to want such affectional reactions and has, accordingly, acquired a new, or secondary drive.

Writing from this position, social psychologist Allison Davis has pointed out that a parent, capitalizing largely on a child's helplessness to satisfy his basic needs by himself, arouses anxiety by withholding approval or giving disapproval or meting out punishment. Thus, the parent contributes to the socialization process by manipulating the mediating process of anxiety. The child learns a myriad of secondary, socially oriented drives that reflect the behavior pattern of his culture as communicated to him largely by his parents. He may, for instance, learn to want to achieve and to be liked, as well as other motivational patterns and values. He also learns the acceptable routes for reducing these acquired drives. The basic theme of SRAL theory is that we are born with certain physiological needs and upon this inborn structure are built learned patterns of motivation that result from social experience.

Freud also recognized the innate quality of the basic physiological needs such as hunger, thirst, sleep, defecation, and urination. But he did not regard these particular physiological needs as especially critical in producing variations in personality structure. To him other inborn needs had paramount importance, for example, sex and aggression. Freud's whole theory of personality was built around the transformations that take place in the sexual and aggressive instincts as the fruit of man's growing up and living in a social world.

Actually, sex is part of a group of instincts that Freud identified as the *life instincts,* a group that included other somatic sources, such as hunger and thirst. But sex is the overriding one in the development of neurotic disorders. The instinct of aggression is an aspect of a second category, the *death instincts.* More recent psychoanalytic writers, however, have tended to abandon the concept of the death instinct, instead deriving destructive behavior out of the thwarting of the sexual instincts.

The life instincts contribute to the survival of the person and of the species through the creation of offspring. The *libido* represents the energy for the life instincts and is concentrated primarily in the various erogenous zones of the body; although any part of the body can be a focus of sexual activity, some areas of the body are especially sensitive to excitation and so produce particularly pleasurable feelings when stimulated. The chief erogenous zones are the lips, the mouth, the anal region, and the primary and secondary sexual organs.

The behavior of the human infant is organized in Freudian theory around the *pleasure principle,* a concept like tension reduction. This is the inherent tendency to obtain immediate pleasure or reduction of pain where possible by the direct discharge of instinctual energy. Thus, for example, sexual energy must be instantly discharged to avoid tension. The discharge will normally occur through various motor reflex actions that are automatic and inherited, or, when this is not possible, through the *primary process* which means the forming of an image or hallucination of an object normally able to permit discharge. In other words, a sexually aroused person learns through experience to conjure up a mental image of an appropriate sex object (usually a member of the opposite sex), and through the primary process he forms a memory image of that object, which is called a *wish fulfillment*.

One concrete example of wish fulfillment was provided in the fantasy behavior of men participating during World War II in militarily sponsored experiments on the effects of semi-starvation. For many weeks volunteers engaged in full-time physical labor while being fed a diet severely reduced in caloric value to a level far below what active men normally require. Some rather interesting personality effects of this semi-starvation were noted, including tremendous preoccupation with food, the placing of food "pin-ups" on the walls of the barracks showing juicy steaks and other appetizing dishes, and determination to change vocations in favor of food-oriented occupations such as cook or restaurateur. We might well regard these activities as examples of primary-process wish fulfillment: The chronic and powerful craving for food led the men to the search for images of food objects ordinarily capable of reducing hunger-induced tension. Hallucinations in mentally disturbed patients, as well as distortions of perception in normal people, are commonly thought to be instances of this primary-process conjuring up of images of satisfying objects.

The trouble with the primary process is that many times we cannot discharge libido directly and immediately because reflex actions are not possible, either due to the inhibition of social forces (as in toilet discipline in the young child) or the unavailability of the actual object (as opposed to the fantasized object) which is required to produce discharge. In this event, wish fulfillment in fantasy will fail to actually reduce the tension. Thus, delay or thwarting of gratification takes place, and from this emerge, in the developing child, the *reality principle* and the *secondary process*. As a result of the delay or thwarting, the ego (one of the mental structures) is created, which operates according to the reality principle and by means of the secondary process. It must do two things. First, it must protect the person against external dangers while, secondly, it must simultaneously make possible the discharge of tension by gratification of the instincts. The ego must evaluate the environmental situation to determine whether instinct-discharge is possible and safe, and to locate the necessary objects to permit such discharge.

In doing these things the ego must be capable of inhibiting the expression of instincts until a safe, satisfying object is found. The reality principle therefore requires the postponement of immediate gratification that is likely to produce pain in order to yield later gratification safely. Freud felt that all complicated mental activities, such as learning, perception, memory, and reasoning, are functions of the ego. The ego structure, by following the reality principle and utilizing the secondary process, inhibits direct instinctual discharge and finds substitute or transformed methods of gratification.

In normal human activities there are many examples of the operation of the secondary process with its inhibition of direct and immediate discharge of tension. The toilet behavior that evolves from infancy to later childhood and lasts throughout life is one. Defecation must be withheld until the appropriate time and place even though the impulse is for immediate discharge. This requires the capability of control over the anal sphincter muscles, and the cognitive processes necessary to identify social pressures and to discriminate the "proper" thing to do. In a comparable way, anger and the impulse to attack someone must be either inhibited completely or diverted to safe objects and situations. The parent who cannot control his rage toward his child when the child's behavior leads to frustration may wind up beating the child so severely as to cause serious injury and even death. Such cases are continually appearing in the newspapers. They exhibit the failure of secondary-process activity in a disturbed adult, one who is unable to control impulses and perhaps even to foresee, according to the reality principle, the consequences of his actions. Without the constraints against, or postponements of, pleasure characteristic of the secondary process, it is difficult to see how any society could exist. For without these controls people could hardly live together in reasonable harmony and safety.

In a way, Freud also subscribed to the division of motives into those that are inborn and physiological and those that are acquired. Sex provides an example of an inborn physiological force that follows the tension-reduction, or pleasure principle. Motivations to learn, to perceive accurately, and to engage in a wide range of socialized behavior are functions of the ego, and represent the Freudian version of secondary, or social, motives that arise only because the pleasure principle cannot work in all instances so delay of discharge and thwarting are impossible to avoid. A person is born into a society that interferes with the direct gratification of these instincts through the social regulations that are aimed at channeling human instincts into socially acceptable paths. These new, socially acceptable paths constitute learned, social, or secondary motives in a sense similar to those in stimulus-response-associative-learning theory.

Freudian theory implicitly assumes that permitting the instincts free rein would be destructive. Man shares these "bad animal" instincts with lower forms of life. The tale of Dr. Jekyll and Mr. Hyde reflects this philosophy very well. Mr. Hyde is all bad; he is the animal part of man. What makes him all bad? Largely his expression of sexual lust and his gratification of destructive impulses toward others. Thus, sexual and aggressive instincts in Mr. Hyde make him a monster, the very instincts that Freud saw as the inherent part of mankind. So they must be harnessed, controlled, inhibited in order for men to live safely and harmoniously with one another. Society performs the valuable function of placing a rein on these animal instincts so that they may be appropriately channeled. Psychopathology can arise either from failing to control these instincts adequately or from inhibiting them so thoroughly that they continue to build tension within a person and express themselves as neurotic symptoms.

The tension-reduction point of view developed above constitutes one general approach to the problem of human motivation. But there is an alternative approach that makes quite different assumptions about the nature of man. For one thing, the Freudian view has been criticized for being too biological and tending to subordinate the importance of social experience in personality development. So-called Neo-Freudian thinkers have emerged who, to an increasing degree, emphasize the social development of man. Moreover, many of these writers replaced the Freudian sexual and aggressive instincts with another type of motive power. The evolution of this latter point of view is complex, but it has reached current fruition as a school of thought that emphasizes what might be called the force for growth; to this school, man has basically desirable inherent potentialities that are distorted by the unfortunate or destructive experiences of living in a badly designed social world. Although this view began to find some expression in the thinking of early Neo-Freudian theorists such as Jung, Fromm, and Rank, it is best expressed in current personality theory by Carl Rogers and Abraham Maslow.

The Force-for-Growth Model

The central motive in man according to Carl Rogers is the need for *self-actualization*. The implicit notion is that man has an innate urge to grow. Rogers assumes that under appropriate conditions man will express higher values than those embodied in the primitive instincts of self-preservation, avoidance of pain, and the seeking of sensual pleasure as identified by Freud. An example of this force for growth in operation is the adolescent who normally seeks independence and autonomy even though he is safer and more comfortable remaining with his parents. Another is the willingness of a person to jeopardize his comfort and security in order to support an unpopular principle in which he believes. In spite of discomfort, then, an inherent growth process leads a person toward individuation and higher development.

The concept of self-actualization as defined by Maslow is that a person always strives toward realizing his inner potentialities. Maslow identifies a hierarchy of needs and values, ranging from the most primitive, which man shares with lower forms of life, to those that are characteristic of only the most advanced types of organism. The hierarchy of needs in man ranges from the lowest survival needs, like hunger and thirst, to higher needs, including belongingness and love, esteem, and cognitive and aesthetic needs such as a thirst for knowledge and a desire for beauty. According to Maslow, higher needs will not be gratified or permitted expression unless the more potent primitive needs are satisfied.

Thus the force-for-growth philosophy implies that, if he is given the opportunity, man will express his advanced nature. When he does not do so, it is because the social conditions of life continue to require the primitive survival struggle to a degree that prevents the realization of his higher potential. Whereas for Freud, cognitive and aesthetic needs are learned sublimated expressions of the primitive sexual and aggressive instincts and, in fact, come into being because these instincts are inhibited through social living, for Rogers and Maslow, they are inborn qualities whose expression depends not on thwarting but on favorable life circumstances.

We said that the origins of the force-for-growth philosophy of man in personality theory can be found among the Neo-Freudians who increasingly emphasized the social basis of man's personality and who questioned the primacy of the life and death instincts as propounded by Freud. Thus, for example, Jung suggested that in middle life man becomes less dominated by libidinal urges and turns toward more philosophical, spiritual concerns about the meaning of life and his place in the universe. Alfred Adler, too, maintained that man has the natural (inborn) tendency to concern himself with "social interest" and communion with other men. Otto Rank, who comes the closest to being the direct forerunner of the force-for-growth school of thought, argues that the fundamental struggle in man is between the desire for social union and the need to become separate or individuated. The person who is most successful in synthesizing these two opposing tendencies Rank calls "the artist," because he presumably engages in the creative act of simultaneously being at one with other men and remaining a separate, distinguishable individual. In a fashion compatible with these notions, psychoanalyst Erich Fromm has attempted to specify the kind of society that permits the individuation of man while sustaining his need for security and belonging. Having re-examined history since feudal times, he maintains that man has not yet evolved a society that does permit the gratification of these conflicting but inherent needs.

We might note a kind of evolutionary assumption in the force-for-growth point of view, specifically, that as we move from primitive to higher animals, new structures of the brain evolve which introduce new needs and capacities. Man is at the highest end of this phylogenetic scale. Thus, he carries with him many needs and capacities that are not found in lower animals. Self-actualization in man, therefore, requires the gratification of these needs that are high or formed later in the phylogenetic series. Nevertheless, in spite of this phylogenetic assumption, the force-for-growth concept has been criticized as mystical and value-laden, since it flirts so continuously with the evaluation of man in terms of normative judgments of high and low, advanced and primitive, good and bad.

Let us shift now to the third issue on which to compare theories of personality—that is, their position on whether personality is rooted in biological or cultural forces. Since this issue tends to overlap extensively with the other two we have discussed, we only need to consider it briefly.

PERSONALITY AS BIOLOGICALLY OR CULTURALLY DETERMINED

The two extreme positions on this matter are equally untenable: Either that personality, and even culture, unfolds solely as a result of inherited, biologically based dispositions, or that personality is entirely a product of the particular culture a person is born into. But between these two poles lie many gradations, if not of theoretical conviction then at least of the dominant focus of research. What are some of these intermediate positions?

Freud took a stance very close to the biological pole. He assumed that psychosexual development, with its oral, anal, and phallic stages, is the normal, universal, biologically determined pattern of mankind. For instance, it is not social experience—toilet training around the second year of life—that leads a child into the anal period of psychosexual development. Rather, in Freud's view, this progression is a function of physiological maturation.

Another example of such biological determination is the famous idea of the Oedipus complex, which is part of the third, or phallic, stage of psychosexual development. During this stage a boy regards his mother as the primary love object and views his father as a competitor for her attention; thus a family triangle develops. For a girl the pattern is reversed: She identifies her father as the main love object (Electra complex). During the Oedipal struggle the boy hates his father-competitor, and his hatred is a source of great anxiety (castration fear) because his wish that the powerful father be eliminated leads him to imagine paternal retaliation. Later on the boy must give up his mother as a primary sexual object in order to make friends with his father and so be protected from the father's possible wrath. During the phallic stage and before this final resolution, the boy defensively identifies with the father and introjects the father's values in order to avoid the danger of castration. This defensive identification process is the most important source of the superego, or conscience, in Freudian theory. Only when the Oedipus situation has been resolved can castration anxiety be relieved; only then can the boy attach himself to another love object outside the family and so progress to the most mature, genital stage of psychosexual development.

Freud believed that this pattern of psychosexual development, with its Oedipus and Electra complexes, would be universal in all cultures, regardless of superficial diversities. In support of his contention Freud noted the universal taboo against incest, a taboo that is evidently consistent with the theory of the Oedipus complex. It is by virtue of this incest taboo that sons and fathers are not in general and continuous warfare, a condition that is true in the mating pattern of many lower forms of life. Among the seals, for example, the gradually maturing son ultimately challenges the aging bull seal, who might be his father, for the privilege of mating with the available females, one of which is likely to be his own mother.

The main point here is that, for Freud, culture is man's attempt to establish patterns within society that permit him to proceed through the various universal stages of psychosexual development with as little conflict as possible and with acceptable and satisfactory discharge of libido (sexual instinct) at each of the various stages. Thus, the forms of culture that evolve are really expressions of the universal biological laws behind the development of individual personality.

Many anthropologists in recent decades have adopted a Freudian, or modified Freudian, view of personality and culture. For example, the famous cultural anthropologist Abram Kardiner, although somewhat critical of Freud's conception of culture as simply an unfolding of biological potential, nonetheless retained the most important features of the Freudian scheme. Kardiner argued that there are certain principal variations in the form of culture that can be observed among different societies, but that there is a limit to the possible variations because of the biologically determined psychosexual stages of man's personality development. Kardiner saw other factors as potent in determining the details of cultural variation—for example, geographical and economic conditions.

According to Kardiner, to understand the interchange between culture and the developing personality of an individual man we must know the culture's child-rearing practices for handling the universal psychosexual stages. For example, if a culture demanded orderliness, conformity, and neatness of its members and enforced these principles rigidly, this pattern would influence the outcome of the anal stage of child development. The culture would be likely to begin toilet training early, to pursue it severely, and to punish infractions harshly. Such a culture would produce a dramatically different kind of personality from what would develop in a culture whose approach to the toilet-training situation was easygoing and undemanding.

Similarly, we could examine cultures in their handling of feeding (for example, early or late weaning) and its impact on the oral stage of development. In short, in Kardiner's view, cultural variations are important because of how they facilitate, or interfere with, the normal, biologically determined psychosexual progression.

Further over on the culture end of the biology-culture continuum is the position of Erich Fromm; he tends to a greater degree than Freud or Kardiner to regard personality as a product of cultural variation. Cultural variation for Fromm, however, is not important because of its effect on the biologically determined psychosexual stages, but because of its influence on the atmosphere of the parent-child relationship. For example, whether love and affection or coldness and rejection are offered to a child would have an important bearing on how the child handled inherent needs for security and autonomy. Patterns of parental authority are also central in importance. A child's response to an autocratic parent is likely to be either excessive submissiveness to, or complete rejection of, authority.

All three of the theorists—Freud, Kardiner, and Fromm—assume that man does have some inborn nature, with Freud taking the most extreme biologically oriented position on this issue, and even he gives considerable attention to the role of experience in personality development.

Even greater emphasis on the social origins of personality is found among sociologists and social psychologists, who emphasize the concept of *social role* and exhibit little interest in the native biological conditions stressed so much by Freud and the Neo-Freudians. Their units of analysis are the interactions of people and the effects of these interactions on the development of the self. Such interactions are largely governed by the organized social roles of the various cultures. Social institutions are thought to comprise role patterns which prescribe how a person must behave and how he must regard himself. One of the earliest theorists of this persuasion was the sociologist George Herbert Mead, who maintained that when a person, A, initiates any action toward another, B, B's response in turn influences A and contributes to the formation of A's conception of himself. This principle of social interaction is central to the social determination of personality. As Theodore Sarbin, one of the modern protagonists of social-role theory in personality, has put it:

With [Ralph] Linton [a noted social anthropologist], we regard a culture as an organization of learned behaviors and the products of behavior which are shared and transmitted. When analyzed, these behaviors appear to be no more and no less than the ordered *actions* of persons, e.g., "mother feeds infant by forcing premasticated food into its mouth." Moreover, persons are always members of a society (defined as an aggregation of persons with common goals), and these societies are structured into *positions* or statuses or offices. The positions are collections of rights and duties designated by a single term, e.g., mother, village chief, teacher, etc. The actions of persons, then, are organized around these positions and comprise the *roles*. Role and position are conjoined. Roles are defined in terms of the actions performed by the person to validate his occupancy of the position. In sum, all societies are organized around positions and the persons who occupy these positions perform specialized actions or roles. These roles are linked with the position and not with the person who is temporarily occupying the position.

Furthermore, the person is characterized by an internal organization of qualities or dispositions, the residue of an individual's experiences as a participant in the culture. In Linton's analysis this aspect is called *personality* and emphasizes individual differences. In role theory, this internal organization of qualities (traits, attitudes, and habits) is conceptualized as the *self*. The term "personality" is reserved for a broader concept: action systems arising out of the interplay of self and role. (Bracketed comment not Sarbin's. Sarbin, T. R., Role theory. In G. Lindzey, ed., *Handbook of social psychology*. Reading, Mass.: Addison-Wesley, 1954, p. 224.)

The writers who conceive of personality in terms of role theory and the interaction of self and role appear, indeed, to exhibit little interest in man's biological nature. They occupy a position closest to the culture pole on the biology-culture continuum. Yet, while their analysis is made at the level of social interaction rather than biological dispositions, they usually leave room for the universally recognized interplay of biology and culture in the development of personality, just as the more biologically oriented writers always accord some place, however small and underemphasized, to the effects of learned social experience.

ADDITIONAL ISSUES

ON WHICH TO COMPARE PERSONALITY THEORIES

Although we have already treated the most important issues for comparing personality theories, there are, of course, many others. We can only touch on them briefly in the present discussion.

One is the *degree of completeness or elaborateness of the theoretical system*. Some theories attempt to cover every facet of human behavior within an elaborate theoretical system. Others take comparatively halting steps in the direction of systematic development presenting only a few major propositions that deal with only certain aspects of human behavior and experience. Sometimes an author has simply not been able to proceed beyond limited theory, and sometimes his interests never carried him beyond a certain point.

The psychoanalytic theory of Freud is the most extensive theoretical statement about personality available to us today. His system of concepts, although highly controversial and only partly absorbed into academic psychology, has had enormous impact not only on the psychology of personality but also on all the social sciences. Freud was a prolific thinker and writer and he had something to say about almost everything. Although his theoretical efforts began with the neuroses, they extended to normal personality, to personality development, to wit and humor, to literature, to anthropology and sociology, and to problems of human creativity. Many of the other great names in personality theory took off from Freud's original material, attacking some of it, modifying some of it, and adding concepts of their own, but never themselves writing a total replacement for Freudian psychoanalysis. Karen Horney, for instance, wrote several books that criticize and modify Freudian theory, overlap it a great deal, and present some new ideas. Without being in any way as complete or elaborate as her mentor, she was a personality theorist in her own right, even though she leaves many questions unanswered in her writings.

Carl Jung perhaps comes as close as anyone to Freud in elaborateness, agreeing with Freud in part but deviating substantially from the original Freudian scheme in developing his own system called "analytic psychology."

In contrast with Freud and Jung, theorists such as Rogers and Maslow have presented relatively little in the way of theory, offering instead a general frame of reference and a set of limited propositions from which a more elaborate theory can be developed later.

Another point of comparison that we have not touched on in this chapter is the degree of *emphasis on conscious or unconscious processes.* Freud's psychoanalytic theory arose at a time when the leading philosophy of Europe had been that man is the master of his destiny and is a rational animal whom we can best understand by examining the way he reasons. So it is not surprising that the idea of Freud which was perhaps hardest for the culture of his times to swallow was that most of the important determinants of man's behavior are unconscious and nonrational. Freud's interests in dream interpretation and the use of free association were based on the conviction that to understand a person we must get below the surface to those reaches of the personality that are unconscious, to the raw, disguised, primitive instincts that energize and direct behavior. Nevertheless, even though the shift was from the "age of reason" to government by nonrational, instinctive forces, Freud also eschewed the earlier tradition that explained man by mystical forces. He took the position of modern science that all behavior is the product of mechanistic forces that can be formulated by scientific laws.

In recent years psychoanalysis has begun moving away from the extreme concern with the primitive unconscious processes of the id and has again turned to an interest in ego function, that is, in the adaptive processes of the personality by which we perceive, learn, and think. Thus, modern ego psychology, while accepting the Freudian premises of the unconscious dynamic factors in the personality, is rediscovering the rational aspects of the human being as well. With the Freudian revolution accomplished and the doctrine of the unconscious determination of behavior widely accepted, it is now possible to take a more moderate position on the rational, adaptive determinants of behavior. Current theories can be compared, then, on the extent of their emphasis on either unconscious, irrational, motivational factors or conscious, adaptive, cognitive processes.

In the present chapter and some of the previous ones we have been concerned chiefly with what personality is like, its main characteristics, and how different theorists have conceptualized it. We have viewed personality contemporaneously, that is, in terms of its current organization. We must now turn to another aspect of personality—its development. Having considered what personality is, we now turn to the question of how it got that way.

The Development
of Personality

When we say that personality develops, we imply an orderly sequence of changes in its structure. Thus, when we have identified a particular structure—for example, a particular motivational pattern or control characteristic—we can attempt to trace its emergence and evolution from infancy on. By development, we usually refer, though, to the early periods of life—starting with infancy, through childhood, to somewhere in young adulthood—because it is during those times that most of the structures of personality emerge and take form. But lately interest has been increasing in the stages beyond young adulthood because

73

6

of the proliferation of practical social problems connected with aging. The structures of personality are, in fact, continually evolving and changing. And even though in later life these changes are apt to be marginal and slow, developmental psychology logically must concern itself to some extent with changes over the whole spectrum of life.

We can approach development in two ways. In *formal developmental theory,* we are preoccupied only with describing and cataloging systematic changes through time in certain characteristics. Alternatively, we can attempt to identify the actual conditions that influence the changes. In the former approach, we usually assume that certain types of orderly change have the status of biological laws. Embryologists, for instance, by investigating babies born prematurely at various ages, have demonstrated that the human fetus proceeds through definite stages in the organization of its response to local stimulation of the face. At a very early stage it reacts with a diffuse, total body response to stimulation by a stiff hair. In later periods the response becomes more and more differentiated so that ultimately, as the fetus approaches full maturity, the response becomes highly localized and specific with only the face muscles reacting to the stimulation. Thus, fetal development demonstrably includes a progression through certain neuromuscular stages that displays the characteristics of a universal biological law.

In psychology, similar principles of development have been postulated by various theorists. Some, such as Heinz Werner, have argued that cognitive development proceeds from a global, diffuse stage to increased differentiation, or specialization, of functions, ultimately reaching a high degree of integration. Many kinds of behavior exemplify this proposed universal biological law. A very young child, for example, is apparently unable to differentiate objects in his environment, such as furniture and people, from one another and from himself. Only gradually does he recognize persons as distinct from things. Eventually, of course, he differentiates and identifies individuals and their various moods, and ultimately he conceives of himself as distinct from the other selves about him. This sort of development is shown in Figure 7, which graphs the increase, with age, of detail responses to the Rorschach Inkblot Test. In that test, a subject is asked to say what each of ten complex inkblots look like. In giving "detail" responses, he selects some part of the blot in constructing his percept, thus differentiating segments of the environment.

Another influential developmental psychologist, Jean Piaget, made a similar analysis. He noted, for example, that children perceive the moon as moving with them as they walk, which suggests the fusion of self and the world that characterizes the immature child. Similarly, a youngster may be perfectly able to identify his right from his left hand but unable to judge hands correctly in another person who is facing him, because, at early stages of development, he cannot separate himself from other objects and imagine himself turned about in space. His apprehension of space is egocentric, as

Piaget termed it—that is, it is based on the orientation of his own body to the world. Only later is he able perceptually to align things in space independently of his own body position.

We may observe other similar changes in patterns of behavior that seem to indicate universal processes of cognitive development. For one, the capacity to control impulses is clearly lacking in an infant or young child: he instantaneously does and says exactly as he feels or wishes. If he is interested in exploring and manipulating a fine piece of china lying on the coffee table, he does so without inhibition. The capacity to exercise control over his impulses normally increases systematically and, as we have noted, is one of the essential qualities of the adult personality. But failure of impulse control sometimes occurs in certain types of adult psychopathology. Indeed, a person may act destructively to himself or others because of his lack of impulse control. In such a case, we assume, something has gone wrong in the normal process of development or there has been regression to an immature stage.

The formal developmental approach to personality, then, is characterized by the search for

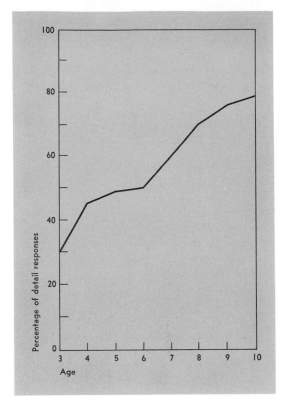

Figure 7. The increase in the percentage of perceptual-detail responses on the Rorschach test with increasing age. (From Hemmendinger, L. Developmental theory and the Rorschach method. In Rickers-Ovsiankina, Maria A., ed., Rorschach psychology. New York: Wiley, 1960, p. 65.)

universal sequences of growth and the description of the processes involved in them. In general, those who pursue this approach are not concerned with the empirical causes or conditions of development. They do not ask, for example, what genetic, physiological, or social factors accelerate, or retard, or distort the development of impulse control in the growing child. Rather, they simply attempt to specify what the stages are and how the structures develop and change.

The second approach, which in effect supplements the formal orientation, attacks the *empirical conditions that influence developmental changes.* These are the factors, biological or social, that contribute to the developmental process by activating, facilitating, or retarding it.

We can draw an example of the distinction between these approaches from

Freud's theory of psychosexual development, which we have already discussed. Formally, this theory postulates universal stages of development that are inferred from the patterns of behavior children exhibit during the first four or five years of life. According to the theory, this progression occurs normally because it is a biological law.

But Freud also paid attention to some of the social conditions that might disturb or retard the normal progression. He maintained that extreme overindulgence or underindulgence during any of the stages would have damaging effects on psychosexual development. For example, if a mother continually overindulged a child in his need for oral gratification by continuing to feed him at the breast long after he should have been weaned, progression to the next (anal) stage of psychosexual development would be inhibited. This inhibition of advancement might be furthered by traumatic experiences associated with the anal period, such as excessively severe toilet discipline. While some of the libido would move ahead to the anal stage, large amounts of libidinal energy would remain fixated at the oral level for the remainder of the individual's life, and he would display certain psychological concomitants of this fixation.

Excessive dependency, Freud assumed, reflects fixation produced by oral overindulgence. Even in adulthood, an orally fixated individual would continually expect oral sustenance in the form of psychological support and aid from others just as he was overindulged in infancy. Excessive underindulgence, in contrast to overindulgence, would also lead a person throughout later life to a perpetual search for oral-type gratifications because he had never fully received them in infancy. Yet even though, in the former case, an attitude of optimism and passive dependency would be entailed, in the latter, the history of frustration would engender pessimism, aggressiveness, and suspiciousness. In this way, with the concepts of trauma and fixation, Freud supplemented his formal theory of psychosexual development in an effort to specify the social conditions that would affect or alter it.

The empirical conditions that influence development can be divided, for convenience, into two general classes. One comprises *physiological factors,* the other, *social factors.* Let us consider each of these classes separately.

PHYSIOLOGICAL FACTORS IN PERSONALITY DEVELOPMENT

We shall discuss physiological factors in personality in two sections. One deals with the relatively new field of behavior genetics, which concerns the role of inheritance in producing a physiology that influences behavior (and, by extension, personality), the other with the direct relations between physiology and behavior. We shall begin with genetics.

Genetics and Personality

The awareness of inheritance on the part of man is extremely old; indeed, many thousands of years before Christ, dogs and other animals were domesticated and probably bred for certain characteristics. In modern times eminent scientists like Charles

Darwin and Francis Galton have believed that even behavioral characteristics as well as physical attributes have a genetic basis. For example, Darwin wrote:

So, in regard to mental qualities, their transmission is manifest in our dogs, horses, and other domestic animals. Besides special tastes and habits, general intelligence, courage, bad and good temper, etc., are certainly transmitted. With man, we see similar facts in almost every family; and we now know through the admirable labors of Mr. Galton that genius, which implies a wonderfully complex combination of high faculties, tends to be inherited; and, on the other hand, it is, too, certain that insanity and deteriorated mental powers likewise run in the same families. (Darwin, *Expression of the emotions in man and animals.* New York: Appleton-Century-Crofts, 1873, vol. 1, pp. 106–107.)

But since the time of Darwin and Galton, systematic efforts at discovering the role of genetics in behavior have not been very successful, as yet, in locating clear mechanisms of genetic effect. This is in contrast to great progress in the genetics of biological structures. Most students of behavior genetics have tried to show that there is a genetic contribution, but few have bent their efforts to identifying the inherited physical structures that contribute to the behavioral characteristics involved. Although there is a widespread, near-universal acceptance of the idea that genetic factors contribute to behavior, the work in this field remains rudimentary. A great deal of it, of course, is concerned with animal behavior. But some labors have been devoted to investigating the genetics of human behavior. Let us consider some of the methods that have been applied and indicate a few findings, especially as they apply to personality characteristics.

The Family Biography. The earliest work, which attempted to show that certain characteristics run in families and are therefore, by inference, inherited, made use of the *family biography,* or the pedigree, method. Galton's own research, which surveyed a number of different families for evidence of a hereditary basis to genius, belonged to this type.

The oft-cited study of the "Jukes" family published in 1875 is another case in point. In examining prison records, the author, Richard Louis Dugdale, a sociologist, was impressed with the persistent appearance of a particular family name and he was led to investigate this family under the pseudonym "Jukes." A high proportion of the Jukeses showed such undesirable characteristics as mental defect, intemperance, and criminality. Interestingly enough, however, Dugdale was more struck by the importance of environment than inheritance in determining the status of the members of the family, a reaction which shows that the family-biography technique can be used to support almost equally well a hereditary or environmental interpretation.

The study some years later (in 1912) of the Kallikak family by psychologist Henry Goddard is another frequently cited family biography. The interesting feature of this study is the contrast it affords in two lines descending from the same man. Martin Kallikak had an illegitimate son in an affair with a feeble-minded girl. This formed one branch of the family, most of whose members were feeble-minded or antisocial in one form or another. Kallikak later married a girl from a good family and in this branch spawned an adequate, normal population of descendants. For years this study was presumed to shed some light on the influence of heredity on behavior.

But the problem with the family-biography approach, even with the two-pronged Kallikaks, is that it is really impossible to separate hereditary and environmental influences. The approach fails because undesirable parents bring up their children in unsatisfactory conditions. Therefore, even if their genetic legacy is somewhat tainted, the situation in which the descendants are reared is also likely to be defective and could in itself be responsible for adjustive failures. The point is clear if we simply reflect on the probable rearing of Kallikak's illegitimate son by the feeble-minded girl and on how he, in turn, would raise his legitimate children, and so on, to further descendants. It is simply impossible to identify here the respective roles heredity and environment have played.

In order to remedy some of the defects of the family-biography technique other methods have been devised. For a complete survey of this area the reader should seek more complete surveys as indicated in the selected readings at the end of this volume. In this discussion we shall touch only on some of the highlights.

Studies of Twins.   Researchers attempting to isolate heredity from environment have turned to studies of twins, in particular to the theoretically ideal *co-twin control* method invented by Galton. This technique requires studying identical twins who have been reared apart under different environmental conditions. One difficulty, of course, is that instances of identical twins reared apart are few and far between, and even the rare examples have often been separated late in childhood or placed in environments that are fairly similar. Another is that it is harder than it was formerly believed to determine whether twins are really identical. Ideally, the co-twin control method properly administered should hold genetic factors constant (identical twins have identical heredity) and permit the isolation of the effects of environmental variation. The converse of this approach, holding environmental factors constant and varying heredity, is technically almost impossible to bring about.

Despite the relative rarity of opportunity, a number of persons have undertaken studies of identical twins—investigating behavioral characteristics such as intelligence as well as physical factors such as height, weight, and incidence of disease—after the twins have been separated and placed in foster homes by public welfare agencies. They all have tended to unearth great similarities among the separated identical twins in the incidence and patterns of diseases, in the presence of glandular disorders, and often even in the results of intelligence tests. For children who had been tested on intelligence before adoption and then studied after some time in a foster home, intellectual functioning remained similar between twins in spite of the environmental variation. Yet especially when environmental variations are extreme, there were also changes. These changes were least evident in physical characteristics and most evident in behavioral characteristics such as intelligence-test performance.

In extreme instances of environmental variation, the higher-scoring twin had invariably received considerable educational and cultural advantages as a result of the foster placement. One study reports on a woman who had an I.Q. of 116 and was a college graduate, although her identical twin had an I.Q. of 92 and had no schooling beyond the second grade. Here is a case where, in spite of identical inheritance, twins differed strikingly in intellect, presumably as a result of altered and unequal environmental circumstances.

Psychological literature in general has in fact, documented the considerable influence of both genetics and environmental circumstances on behavior. Thus, we can more fruitfully attack the question of heredity versus environment if we recognize at once that they interact in producing behavioral characteristics. Both factors can be influential, and their relative importance depends on the degree of variation in both and the characteristic being studied. So far though, heredity-environment studies have come to grips with the problem of personality characteristics infrequently and then only with relatively meager techniques of personality assessment.

One variation on the twin approach to heredity and environment in personality has been employed extensively by geneticist Franz Kallman in the study of hereditary factors in schizophrenia and other psychoses. Kallman's variation is called the *method of concordance* because it predicts the likelihood that one member of a sibling pair will have a specified condition (for instance, schizophrenia) when it is known that the other member is sick. Comparing the index of concordance among identical twins, fraternal twins, full siblings, and half siblings, makes it possible to infer the hereditary component in a particular pathology. This is so because, in identical twins, the hereditary factor is strong, whereas in fraternal twins and in full siblings it is less potent, though more so than in half siblings.

Essentially, Kallman's method is this: He digs through hospital records of schizophrenic, manic-depressive, or involutional melancholia patients to identify those who have an identical twin, fraternal twin, full sibling, or half sibling. He then seeks to determine the condition of that twin or sibling. The index of concordance is simply the percentage of times that the second half of the pair has the same pathology as the first, after the first one has been identified as such from the hospital records. Kallman reports that the index of concordance for identical twins is dramatically higher than that for fraternal twins, which in turn is higher than that for half sibs and unrelated pairs of individuals. Figure 8 presents Kallman's data on concordance for three types of psychosis and for the several types of genetic relationship.

Kallman does not hold that the various disorders studied are directly inherited but rather that genetic factors dispose a person to become sick. In support of his position, he cites similar data for tuberculosis. A person cannot become tubercular unless he comes in contact with the disease-producing bacteria. Thus, the disease cannot be directly inherited, only the disposition or lack of resistance to the illness can. The same argument is offered for schizophrenia and other psychoses. If a person has a strong genetic disposition to respond to life stress with schizophrenia and he is exposed to the appropriate environmental conditions, the illness will occur. What the disposition consists of physiologically Kallman does not suggest, but he thinks his data offer good evidence that we should look for the genetic and physiological seeds of psychosis.

Kallman's research remains highly controversial. Indeed, it has been bitterly criticized by psychologists interested in the etiology of mental illness.

The
Development
of Personality

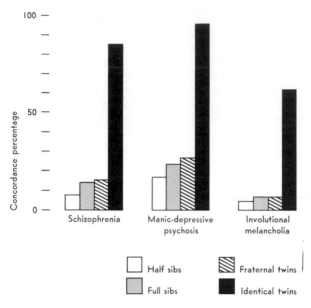

Figure 8. Indexes of concordance established by Kallman for various mental disorders. (From Kallman, F. J. Heredity in health and mental disorder. *New York: Norton, 1953, p. 124, fig. 36.*)

Some object—and the probability that this is so is strong—that Kallman severely exaggerated the concordance rates for identical twins, although it is not clear to what extent methodological inadequacies vitiate the data altogether. Some researchers even argue that the findings are uninterpretable because of these methodological errors. For one thing, the method of concordance has weaknesses, since environmental factors may not be entirely ruled out. The environments of identical twins may be more similar than those of fraternal twins, for instance, since parents are acutely conscious of identicalness and since twins too tend to regard themselves as identical, to dress alike, and to react similarly. Thus, the high incidence of concordance could be due in large part to this uniform environment.

In addition, the same person who obtained the records of mental illness, Kallman, also determined whether the second of a pair showed evidence of sickness. This would pose a sticky problem when the second person was not actually hospitalized and judgment had to be exercised about the extent of his psychopathology. Since Kallman knew of the original classification and had strong convictions about the role of genetics, he may have unwittingly exaggerated the incidence of concordance. These and other problems make his interpretation of genetic factors in psychopathology open to serious question. The data are more likely to be accepted by psychologists who favor the genetic and physiological approach to behavior, than by those who are environmentally or socially oriented. A definitive study using the concordance method remains to be done.

The Concept of Instinct. Personality psychologists do not normally turn to the methods and findings of genetics in tracking down the origins of personality, although they often tend to assume that personality must be at least a partial product of genetic factors. One place in personality theory, though, where the assumption of genetic influences is central, is the concept of instinct. Instinct has long been a highly controversial term in psychology, especially when it is used in the worst sense of merely being a label for phenomena we want to explain. For example, to say that men fight with each other because of the instinct of aggression is to engage in circular reasoning rather than to explain destructive behavior. Such a statement does point toward a genetic, physiological explanation of aggression that would be useful if a precise mechanism could then be further identified. But no one has done this so far, and too little is known about neurophysiology even to make the effort at the present time.

Still, the conviction persists among many personality theorists that certain dispositions are indeed part of man's physical structure and that while these dispositions and their forms of expression are modifiable, genetic factors common to the species produce them. The personality researcher is impressed, for example, that aggression is the most prepotent response to frustration and that it is difficult for human beings to learn other reactions. Although man does have to learn the form in which to express his anger—whether to attack physically, make barbed verbal assaults, demolish the enemy through organized social channels like war, or inhibit the aggression and perhaps even turn it upon himself as in self-criticism and suicide—the assumption is widespread that the impulse originates in universally inherited dispositions.

Freud made extensive use of a modified concept of instinct, and Maslow, whom we met earlier in relation to the force-for-growth point of view, attempts to make a case for the concept of "instinctoid needs," needs that have instinctual origins but that may be inhibited or transformed in expression by social experience. In any event, the concept of instinct in the field of personality contains an inherent problem of behavior genetics, and further research on the latter subject may teach us to ask the proper questions that will throw light on the former.

We turn now to the physiological factors themselves that are an integral part of behavioral variations and, by extension, personality.

Human Physiology and Personality

If physiology does contribute to behavior, then it is also a factor in the intervening structures and processes of personality. As we compare characteristic behavior in organisms throughout the phylogenetic series, we find that behaviors are similar when neurological structures are alike and dissimilar when the nervous systems are structurally different. When we get to man, the job of relating physical structure to psychological function becomes complex and subtle. This is especially true in the area of individual differences in behavior, which is, of course, the empirical subject matter of the field of personality.

In the present discussion, we are assuming that differences in behavior under the same circumstances (and hence differences in personality) are associated with either anatomical differences or differences in the functioning of body tissues. The relationships between physical structure and psychological function, especially for so complex a concept as personality, are extremely difficult to identify. In fact, most of the pertinent work in this area deals with far simpler forms of behavior than the personality psychologist is usually interested in. But it is reasonable to expect that first progress along these lines will be made in the sector of the simple forms of behavior before it is extended into areas more directly pertinent to personality itself.

The problem of the physiological bases of behavior is large and complex. Our concern here is the relationship between physiology and behavior that is germane to personality. It is relevant to point out that we can study the influence of physiological factors on behavior in two ways. One is to create temporary physiological states experimentally and observe their behavioral effects, and the other is to examine stable differences among people in glandular, neurological, or other organ structures that might be possible correlates of variations in behavior.

In recent years the use of drugs that produce certain effects on the nervous system and hence on behavior has become an important and well-established tool of physiological psychology. In personality research, drugs such as lysergic acid or mescaline are used because they appear capable of producing hallucination-like experiences that have a certain superficial similarity to those found in psychotic disorders like schizophrenia. It is the hope of many psychopharmacologists that they can understand the mechanisms of such disorders by analogy if they can learn how these drugs affect the nervous system. In this way they will be able to guess what goes wrong in the cell metabolism of the brain, for example, in the psychotic individual. Thus, while the socially oriented psychologist is attempting to understand psychological functioning and malfunctioning in terms of disturbances in social relations, the physiological psychologist is concerned with explaining these disorders at the level of physiological structure and function.

Physiological factors can affect behavior either directly or indirectly. In *direct influence,* normal behavior is altered by damage to tissues or by structural or functional conditions in the nervous system. For example, metabolic disturbances that result from inadequate functioning of the endocrine gland system may produce many behavioral effects, such as hyperactivity, sluggishness, and reported anxiety. Damage to the brain from physical injuries or diseases such as syphilis can produce impairment in adaptive behavior and marked changes in a person's relationship with other people. There is no doubt that these disturbances are definitely produced by damage to the brain tissue, although the mechanism whereby the damage is reflected in behavior is not entirely clear and will not be fully understood until the precise relationship between brain physiology and psychological functions is clearly comprehended.

Indirect influences occur when the physiological conditions involved do not produce a specific behavioral effect but have social consequences that in turn affect the individual so that his behavior is altered. A physical handicap is a striking example of indirect influence because it may produce negative or disturbed reactions in other people. Their reactions may cause the handicapped individual to feel inadequate, to attempt to compensate for the defect, perhaps to withdraw from social contacts, or to resort to one of a variety of other adjustments. A girl who is unattractive may develop an insecure or compensating personality strongly influenced by this physical fact. Similarly, a child endowed with considerable physical strength and large stature will discover in playing with other children that he is stronger than they, so he may develop a different personality from that of a lad who is sickly and puny.

We must always regard the effects of physiological factors on personality as being equally dependent on social factors. That is, it is the interaction of the two that determines the end product we call personality. The problem of sorting out influences is the same one we faced earlier with heredity and environment. Research into the physiological and social origins of the development of personality, however, has given relatively little attention to these interactions. The physiological psychologist inclines toward the isolated study of physiological variables, and the socially oriented psychologist conversely addresses himself primarily to the analysis of social influences. This is true even though personality theorists of either persuasion are continually and validly assuming their interplay.

One good way to reveal the influence of physiological processes on personality-relevant behavior is to take the central constructs of personality and consider what psychologists have been thus far able to demonstrate about their physiological basis. Since researchers have more and more aimed at exploring the physiological component of motivation and emotion and of the higher adaptive processes of cognition, let us see what evidence on those constructs they have been able to adduce.

The Physiology of Motivation and Emotion.   The great bulk of research on the physiology of motivation has dealt not with the complex social motives in which personality theorists are interested, but with the simpler, so-called primary drives universal to all animals, such as hunger, thirst, and sex. It is at present an article of faith that understanding the physiology of these motivations will promote comparable understanding of the physiology of social motivations. The usual assumption is that the laws governing one will turn out to be applicable, in the main, to others. At any rate, most of what we now know of these social matters comes from the study of the basic drives.

It was once thought that motivated behavior, such as activity to assuage hunger, derives from the local activities of the appropriate organ, in this case the stomach. Thus, contractions of the stomach, it was held, produce discomfort or tension; the animal then discovers that eating food reduces these painful sensations. Some experiments supported this concept, but other evidence soon developed which showed that even in the absence of stomach sensations (the stomach being removed by surgery) hunger nonetheless occurred.

A more modern and complex physiological theory of motivation has been recently developed. According to this new approach, the physiology of motivation is a highly complex affair, dependent on the regulation of sensations from the viscera by the central nervous system, by chemical characteristics of cells and of the blood, by activities of the cerebral cortex, and especially by neurological centers in the hypothalamus. This latter organ is a specialized group of tissues in the mid-part of the brain that has received increasing importance in the physiology of motivation and emotion.

One recent theory asserts that a *central motive state* is built up by combined sensory, humoral, and neural influences and that the hypothalamus is the main integrating center. An appreciable amount of research shows that damage to certain portions of the hypothalamus produces striking changes in certain types of motivated behavior. For example, damage to very specific areas produces enormous overeating in a rat, leading the animal to double his body weight, whereas damage to the specific area only a few millimeters away will completely eliminate hunger so that the animal never eats again and dies.

This research has fostered the proposal that both excitatory centers and inhibitory centers exist in the hypothalamus of the brain. Excitatory centers generate motivated behavior, whereas inhibitory centers terminate it. If you destroy the inhibitory center for hunger, an animal eats incessantly. If you destroy the excitatory center for hunger, the animal never eats. A similar pattern has been found for sleep, and at least an excitatory center for sex has been located.

Just as there appear to be excitatory and inhibitory hypothalamic areas, so there are areas which control different kinds of motivation. The evidence is that the destruction of one area will produce behavioral effects related to hunger, another will affect thirst, and so on, for sleep and sex. Clearly, there is considerable specialization of function in the different structural parts of the hypothalamus.

The relationship between the processes of motivation and those of emotion is so extremely close that the two concepts have generally been regarded as practically inseparable. As it is with motivation, the hypothalamus is the main regulatory center of emotional behavior, too. In addition to the hypothalamus, higher centers such as the cerebral cortex also contribute to the arousal and inhibition of emotional states, just as they do for motivation.

Besides these brain centers, the *autonomic nervous system* also plays an important role in emotion. This role has been known for a long time because the autonomic nervous system serves most of the visceral organs such as the heart, lungs, and gastrointestinal tract—and these organs are known to respond actively during mild as well as severe emotional states. Thus, during emotion we experience changes in heartbeat, the rate and amplitude of breathing, and many other internal changes that people have long associated with aroused states of feeling.

One intriguing problem is whether we can differentiate emotional states in terms of autonomic response patterns, that is, whether we can specify what particular organs respond in given emotions—say, fear or anger—and how. It was once thought that the autonomic physiological patterns of fear and anger were indistinguishable. Evidence is now beginning to turn up, however, that the reactions of the autonomic nervous system in these two states, although overlapping considerably, do differ. This concept is partly borne out by the common-sense observation that in fear a person becomes pale and has a dry mouth, whereas anger causes no such drying of the mouth and often produces a noticeable redness in the face. Apparently, then, the patterns of response in circulation as well as salivation are quite distinguishable in these two strong emotional conditions. Recent experimental work lends support to the case for separate physiological correlates of different emotions.

What is perhaps most interesting in this area is the possibility that, because of either genetic factors or experience, or a combination of the two, individuals may develop particular physiological traits that produce slightly differing physiological responses in the same emotional state. And it is also intriguing to consider the possibility that patterns of psychosomatic symptoms might vary to some extent from person to person depending on these constitutional traits that show up in their reactions to the stresses of life.

Our consideration of the physiology of motivation and emotion has tended to keep to the nervous system, which is, of course, the focal point of a large share of the research in this area. It is also important, however, to mention the function of the *endocrine gland system* in the control of emotion. While the autonomic nervous system is rapidly stimulating the organs of the body in emotional states and the sensory nerves are undoubtedly passing on to higher nervous centers information about this activity, secretions of the endocrine glands serve to sustain these reactions, often long after the crisis that generated the emotion in the first place has passed. Thus, the central medulla portion of the adrenal gland secretes adrenalin and noradrenalin into the bloodstream, each of which produces particular effects on the visceral organs. We should always remember that emotional states, like motivations, are complex matters involving hormonal substances, the nerve pattern of the autonomic nervous system, the activation of centers of the hypothalamus, and regulation by higher brain centers such as those of the cerebral cortex.

Just as variations in physiological functioning influence patterns of motivated and emotional behavior, so they must influence the stable characteristics of personality. It is well known that every human being has a unique nervous system; presumably the cellular activity of this nervous system is unique, too. Thus, it is altogether reasonable to assume that these subtle differences can have a strong impact on personality and account partly, in interaction with social experience, for the variations in personality that we observe.

The Physiology of Cognitive Processes.   The methods and problems connected with the physiology of cognition are similar to those connected with motivation and emotion. Here the focal point of research for the past century and a half has been the brain. Once psychologists recognized in the 1800's that the brain was the central organ of adaptation, they launched attempts to correlate specific psychological functions with particular areas of the brain, an activity since called *brain mapping*.

The aim in brain mapping is to identify specific organs or structures within the brain and to associate these organs with particular classes of behavior. We have seen an example of this process in the identification of the hypothalamus as a control center in motivation and emotion. But a running controversy has existed for a long time about how sharply localized, if at all, psychological functions are within areas of the brain. Researchers generally accept that some localization of function exists even though it is not nearly so precisely articulated as was once believed. This is especially true of the cerebral cortex, the outer rim of the brain, with its convolutions, the parts of which have been associated with different types of adaptive functioning. For example, some areas of the cortex, it has been shown, relate mainly to auditory perception, whereas others appear to control and coordinate visual functions, motor functions, and so forth. In man it is also clear that brain lesions produced by accident or tumor may have serious effects on memory as well as on sensory processes.

The extensive work being done on the effects of damage to the cerebral cortex on cognitive behavior is part of a continuing systematic effort to study the physiological structures (primarily neurological) that are associated with adaptive psychological functions such as perception, memory, and thinking. Comparable efforts are being directed at the relationship between brain waves and attentiveness and at the relationship between adaptive behavior and brain chemistry. The latter involves the study of enzymes in brain cells and metabolic activity in brain tissue.

Clearly, research on the physiology of motivation, emotion, and cognition is new and incomplete, and we have presented examples of it here merely to illustrate the direction of this effort. But it is not just an intellectual diversion, for the psychologist concerned with personality hopes that ultimately these studies will provide evidence of the physiological factors in the stable processes of motivation and control that make up personality. Still, we must always remember that the physiological construction of man represents only one class of factors in the development of personality. Now let us see about the influence of social factors.

SOCIAL FACTORS IN PERSONALITY DEVELOPMENT

In taking on the task of clarifying the role of social factors in personality development, we need to attack two fundamental issues. One is the nature and extent of the influence of social factors on behavior. This is the same sort of issue we met in behavior genetics and in the area of physiological factors in personality. The specific problem here is to determine the effects of growing up in different social contexts. The second issue is more theoretical: how such influence is transmitted. The question is, by what mechanism is social influence on personality development mediated? Let us look into each of these issues in turn.

The Nature of Social Influences on Personality

In tracing the effect of various social institutions on behavior, we may want to start with the broadest dimension of social factors we can find—specifically the cultural pattern taken as a whole, either temporally or spatially. Temporally, it is clear that our cultural patterns have changed and are continually changing so that what was appropriate long ago is no longer appropriate now. For example, fifty years ago women could not vote, were not expected to obtain anything more than a narrowly prescribed education, had great restrictions imposed on their freedom of movement and action, and in general had clearly articulated social roles to play in relation to men—in occupation, in marriage and courtship, and in nearly every other area of social importance. These temporal variations of cultural pattern we can presumably associate with differences in the personality characteristics of people living in these respective times.

Along with variation through time within one culture, we can find variation among cultures spatially—that is, simultaneous cultural differences in different parts of the world. One of the tasks undertaken by cultural anthropologists is the exploration and description of the various cultures of the world.

The value of their work for us is that, by studying personality in diverse places, we can probably identify differences that are attributable to cultural variations.

Anthropologists such as Margaret Mead have performed intensive studies of various primitive societies. One such undertaking, which has thrown light on one of the common phenomena of our own and other societies—the storm and stress of adolescence, is her probing investigation of that developmental period in Samoa. It was once widely assumed that the turmoil experienced by adolescents resulted from the dramatic physiological changes concomitant with growing up, especially alterations in the endocrine glands and the maturation of secondary sex characteristics. Mead discovered, however, that in those societies that provide a harmonious psychological transition between childhood and adulthood, adolescence does not have the disturbing qualities often observed in our own society.

In Samoa, a girl's first menstruation is greeted with celebration. Before puberty she has taken the responsibility for a great many family chores, including assisting in caring for the younger children. And following adolescence when she marries, she must again take on the responsibility of rearing a family, this time her own. But during adolescence she is suddenly free of most responsibility so that she may court, engage in sex play, and prepare to marry. Adolescence in Samoa appears to be blissful for a girl: Her lot in life is clearly defined and she has no evident source of anxiety. Although the study focuses on girls, the implications are that the same is true of boys.

This pattern is in sharp contrast to the plight of an adolescent in our own society: He usually has a difficult time of it psychologically. He is expected to be increasingly independent and responsible, an emergent adult, yet essentially he is still treated as a child who is dependent on his family both psychologically and economically. The adolescent must face the future uncertain of career and economic status if he is a boy, unsure of marriage and social status if she is a girl. It is a period of considerable anxiety about the future and a wrenching away from the past.

Mead has also described the transition from childhood to adulthood among the Arapesh of New Guinea. The shift there is also gradual and easy. Arapesh adults are affectionate, trusting, and unaggressive and are oriented primarily to rearing children and growing food. A boy takes over adult responsibilities very gradually after an easy initiation ceremony. At the age of seven or eight a girl is betrothed to an older boy and goes immediately to live with his family. Her puberty is marked by an initiation ceremony, but little change occurs in her pre-adolescent way of life. Her parents-in-law are highly indulgent to her, and both she and the boy to whom she is betrothed live as members of the same family and community group. With their passage from childhood to adult married life so gradual and benign, Arapesh girls also show little if any emotional disturbance specific to the time of life.

In contrast with the Arapesh and the Samoans, Tchambuli society reveals a pattern of conflict in adolescence more like our own. Boys of nine and ten are forced away from the protection and support of adult women and are expected to take on responsible adult functions. Yet, for a considerable period these boys are not welcomed by the adult males, who consider them unfit. This youthful status of being neither man nor boy generates a great deal of strain, and, in that sense, the pre-adolescent period in Tchambuli society seems to correspond to the adolescent period in our own culture. Such anthropological evidence shows us that cultural variations in social-role patterns seem to produce extensive differences in degree of stress and in characteristics of personality.

But it is not necessary to compare grossly different cultures to observe striking effects of social factors on personality development. We can examine institutional patterns within a society and relate personality variations to them. For example, male and female social roles tend to be sharply differentiated in all societies. In our own culture, although the roles of men and women have altered over the years and more and more tend to overlap, different patterns of behavior are still expected for each sex. These sex-role patterns are usually imposed early in childhood. Thus, toys typically reflect the sex roles that parents expect children to adopt. A girl is given dolls, cosmetics, kitchen equipment, and all such things that reflect the behavior and interests of her mother. Conversely, a boy gets athletic and construction toys—balls, trucks, erector sets, and the like. It is often a cause of distress in parents to find that their son is interested in feminine things or that their girl is a tomboy.

Although certain sex-role patterns are "normal" to us, often quite different ones are the standard in other societies. Cultural anthropologists have discovered some intriguing variations in sex roles in primitive societies which suggest that feminine and masculine behavior is not determined entirely by physiology. Mead observes, for example, that in the Arapesh of New Guinea, women carry supplies from the farming area to the village. With 60-to-70-pound loads hanging from their foreheads, they walk long distances and climb up and down steep paths. This work assignment is considered quite proper by both men and women of the Arapesh since, they point out, "it is appropriate that women should carry heavier loads than men do, because women's heads are so much harder and stronger." Similarly, Arapesh women readily take the initiative in sex and in community affairs along with the men, and little distinction is made between masculinity and femininity in personality. This situation stands in marked contrast to our own society and even more so to the Tchambuli society of New Guinea which appears to reverse our usual conceptions of maleness and femaleness. To the Tchambuli, women are naturally dependable, self-sufficient, and lusty, whereas men are sensitive, vain, and temperamental.

Our description of social influences on the development of personality could be indefinitely extended to include many other institutionalized variations. For example, there is evidence of differences in attitude toward aggression as a function of social class. The lower-class child is encouraged to be physically aggressive and to respect effectiveness in fighting, whereas the middle-class child is taught that physical assault is bad. Concerning the expression of aggression, the middle-class child must learn a complex set of rules that includes the following precepts: Never strike adults and always be respectful toward them; do not attack girls, rather be chivalrous toward them; verbal aggression is better than physical aggression; when attacked or when in a competitive situation give a good account of yourself, but never initiate unwarranted aggressions against another child.

Child rearing practices have been shown to vary in many other ways as a function of social-class membership. Social psychologist Martha Ericson writes of her own research findings which typify work on this problem:

Middle-class families were generally found to be more exacting in their expectations for children with reference to the learning of habits of feeding, cleanliness training, environmental exploration and control, and age- and sex-roles. Training was generally begun earlier in the middle-class than in the lower-class families. In the middle-class families, there was more emphasis on the early assumption of responsibility for the self, closer supervision of children's activities, and greater emphasis on individual achievement. (Ericson, Martha C., Social status and child-rearing practices. In Newcomb, T. M., and Hartley, E. L. *Readings in social psychology.* New York: Holt, Rinehart and Winston, 1947, p. 498.)

This variation among social classes in child-rearing practices with respect to the age at which the child is expected to begin helping at home is illustrated in Table 4, which is taken from Ericson's research.

TABLE 4

Age When Child Is To Begin Helping at Home

Age	Middle-Class Percentage	Lower-Class Percentage
2– 5 years	58.5	35.4
6– 8 years	31.7	45.0
9 years and over	9.8	19.6
Total	100.0	100.0

There is some recent evidence that patterns of child-rearing for the various social classes have changed in the last ten to fifteen years. The general point, however, is still perfectly valid. And these and other extensions of the argument would merely proliferate evidence that social factors do indeed make a difference in personality. We must now turn to the second issue we raised earlier in this section. How do social factors influence personality? That is, what is the mechanism of influence?

How Social Factors Influence Personality

There seem to be two general ways through which society influences the individual. The less important for personality development is *formal* education, the systematic efforts made in most societies to educate new generations of children to their culture by means of books, schools, or formal teaching of one sort or another. The other method is *informal education.* This occurs when the child models his behavior after parents or other significant adults in the society, thus acquiring from them the behavior patterns appropriate to the culture.

Often what a child learns through formal education turns out to conflict with what he discovers through informal means. A child may learn the idea (and the words to express it) that honesty and a humanitarian outlook toward others are to be esteemed. But at the same time he may discover that, in reality, his parents and others respect the conniving individual who manages successfully to take advantage of his fellows. Formally the child learns what he must openly affirm as proper behavior and values, while informally he assimilates the actual values and behavior patterns of parents and parent-substitutes as reflected in their behavior.

In effect, the most important means of transmitting culture (as a personality influence) is the parent-child relationship. One aspect of this relationship is found in the child-rearing practices of the family, which, of course, reflect the culture or the subculture to which the family belongs. But the question of how the process of internalization of the culture by the child occurs still remains to be answered.

Personality theorists offer some answers. Freud, for example, had very definite ideas about how and why introjection takes place. He considered it as part of the process of superego formation. The crucial impetus for the formation of a boy's superego (which contains the conscience and ego-ideal) occurs during the phallic period and is associated with the struggle over the Oedipus complex and its attendant fear of retaliation by the father. This "castration anxiety" leads a boy to seek a benign relationship with his father by denying his sexual interest in the mother and by introjecting the father's values in a process often called defensive identification or *identification with the aggressor*. The supposed reasoning is, if one incorporates the aggressor—the father—by becoming like him, one is likely to be safer from the dangers of retaliation. By conducting oneself irreproachably there is no longer anything to fear. Thus, the boy introjects his image of the father and becomes like him. In the girl a parallel process occurs with respect to her mother. Although present-day psychoanalysts recognize that superego formation begins before the Oedipal problem has developed and can proceed in part independently of it, the attempted resolution of the Oedipus complex is still considered the cornerstone of the internalization of the parents' values.

Another explanation of this internalization is found in the stimulus-response-association-learning frame of reference. Adherents to this view argue compellingly that anxiety is of the utmost importance in the normal process of socialization. Parents manipulate anxiety in a child by rewarding him (with approval or other means) when his behavior conforms to the cultural pattern and by punishing him (with disapproval or other means) when it does not. Disapproval creates anxiety in the child, because it warns that the parents may withhold gratification of primary needs or may even harm him in some way.

Both these explanations stress one essential feature of the parent-child relationship: The *helplessness of the child* and, correspondingly, the *power of the parents*. The parents have enormous importance to the young child because he cannot fend for himself and because they are so clearly the source of all that is beneficial or harmful. Thus, in Freudian theory, a boy fears retaliation from his father because the father is powerful compared to himself; otherwise, why fear retaliation? And in the association-learning analysis, a parent is capable of inducing anxiety because the child depends so thoroughly on him for his safety and security. The Neo-Freudians, too, stress the in-

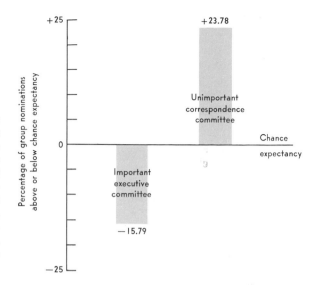

Figure 9. Percentages above and below chance of assignments of "deviate" members by group members to important and unimportant committees. (Adapted from Schachter, S. Deviation, rejection, and communication. J. Abnorm. Soc. Psychol., 1951, 46, 190–207.)

dividual's feeling of helplessness, insecurity, or loneliness, especially when young.

But when the child grows up, parental influence is reduced, as most parents can attest who are still seeking full obedience from an adolescent youngster. By adolescence, the force of power no longer functions so directly and obedience largely depends on what has already been internalized long before. Every parent is familiar with the increasing autonomy, independence, and negativism toward authority that characterize even a young child. The negativism so common in a two-year-old that dismays his parents might also be viewed with satisfaction since it is a sign that an individuated person is being formed. No child can forever be merely a puppet manipulated by parents, or a carbon copy of them, and still be a person in his own right.

Although it is true that some of the power of adults over children is reduced as the child becomes a competent adult, the mature person must still be somewhat beholden to others in the pursuit of his security and satisfaction. This is the reason why the classic study of social conformity pressures on individuals performed by Asch and described in Chapter 1 gave evidence of so much conflict and yielding by the experimental subjects. Each of them was faced with a grave conflict when he found his judgment in opposition to the group. The conflict occurred because, even in adult life, the social group continues to hold some power over the individual's welfare.

In follow-up studies of this problem other psychologists have demonstrated experimentally how this power is reflected in the behavior of the group toward the individual who deviates from the group standards. In one study the person who took an attitude that deviated from the one adopted by the rest of the group was seldom nominated for important committee assignments, and, further, nominated most commonly to unimportant committees, as shown in Figure 9. Moreover, the other members often rated the "deviate" not acceptable as a group member. Although the process of socialization in childhood gets under way because the parent is powerful and the child dependent, throughout life the social group continues to mount pressures toward conformity because the person needs social approval for his well-being.

If we are to study empirically the nature of the social influences in childhood that determine personality, we must look to the parent-child relationship. Even though our knowledge in this regard is quite limited as yet, there are an increasing number of studies that explore the importance of various parental attitudes toward the child. It is, of course, possible to isolate for study many particulars of the parent-child relationship and specific procedures of child-rearing. Among the most common topics are age of weaning, techniques of toilet training, the handling of dependency, efforts to form attitudes toward sex and aggression, the character of parental discipline, rejection, and maternal overprotection. Developmental psychologists are paying increasing attention to comparative analysis, empirical as well as theoretical, of the parent-child relationship and child-rearing practices both among groups within our society and between societies.

At present, on the basis of fairly limited information, psychologists are continually attempting to make educated guesses, not only about the actual effects of social factors on personality development, but also about the mechanisms of such influence. Were final answers to the questions in this area available, we would probably also have precise knowledge of, and control over, the respective factors that lead either to mental health or psychopathology. Great strides along these lines have been made in the short time in which systematic attention has been given to these problems, yet there is still an enormous void in our knowledge and understanding in this area.

In this chapter we have outlined the issues inherent in studying genetic, physiological, and social contributions to the development of personality. But even were these problems resolved, our understanding would still depend on our being able to hew out the real keystone of methodology: the assessment of personality structure. For clearly, if we are to identify the precise influence of various factors on development, then we must be able to measure this thing we call personality. We take up the problem in Chapter 7.

Personality Assessment

To build a theory of personality and to test it requires a well-developed technology of measurement or assessment. Theory specifies the important structures of personality and the rules of their organization and functioning, as we indicated in Chapters 4 and 5. But in a scientific endeavor, the concepts of the theory must also be tied to what is directly observable. We must be able to specify the forms of behavior that identify the existence and operation of the hypothetical structures and processes we are speculating about. To the extent that we can do this successfully, we have a tightly organized science that permits us to un-

7

derstand and predict. Practitioners of the science of personality struggle continually to attain this tight organization, sharpening their concepts about personality so that they will conform to the empirical relationships that are observable in human behavior. To do so, of course, they need valid and reliable procedures of assessment. So let us examine how this process of assessing theoretical constructs works.

THE ASSESSMENT OF THEORETICAL CONSTRUCTS

The best way to tackle the problem is to take some common personality construct and consider briefly how it might be assessed. A good example to work with is the concept of motivation. Personality researchers have proposed many kinds of human motives, motives that vary in strength. In addition to the physiologically based motives that alter with bodily states of deficiency—for example, hunger—there are the more socially oriented motives, such as the desire to succeed against some standard of excellence. This latter has often been called *achievement motivation.*

Postulating differing strengths of achievement motivation in different persons can help us understand how people act in various situations. For an everyday example, when a teacher, in contrasting one student who works with great energy on his academic assignments with another who seems indifferent to his studies, says that the former has a stronger motive to achieve (at least academically), he is making an inference from what he has seen. He is, in other words, informally assessing the student's motivation to achieve on the basis of some directly observable pattern of behavior.

From the point of view of the professional assessment psychologist, it is essential to find classes of behavior that may be used to measure, by inference, the constructs of personality that have previously been created to explain the behavior, and to find evidence that supports or refutes the usefulness of these constructs. In Chapter 3 we dealt with the diverse sources of information from which personality structures and processes are inferred. In assessment procedures and research we also use these sources of information, usually in the form of standardized methods for getting information about a person. These include, as we shall see, the case history, the interview, and the psychological test.

But let us get back to the problem of motivation. We have at our disposal many types of behaviors by which we might measure the degree of a given motive. We can observe how much time and energy a person spends at some kind of activity. We can ask him direct questions about how important certain goals are to him. On the principle that motives are reflected in dreams, daydreams, and other kinds of fantasies, we can create ways of getting at such fantasy material and study how much it reflects a given motive. (Freud suggested just such a role for fantasy in his famous book on the interpretation of dreams.) This latter solution—using fantasy to measure motivation—is, in fact, exactly what some personality-oriented psychologists have attempted, and it will serve here as a concrete example of attempts to assess personality constructs.

During the late 1930's the experimental question was asked whether hungry persons tend to report more images and associations about food than non-hungry persons. Several psychologists performed some pertinent experiments. In one of them, the researcher arranged to have experimental subjects available who had eaten at different intervals during the previous 24 hours, and he tested their associations and images. He found that more food images were given by the hungry subjects than the nonhungry subjects, a finding which lent support to the idea that a motive state would be reflected in associations and fantasies, and therefore, might be measured by them.

There followed a long line of experimental research along these lines, culminating in the extensive studies of David McClelland and his colleagues on the achievement motive. In these studies researchers attempted in various ways to stimulate in their subjects strong needs to achieve. One way they did this was by giving them an experience of failure in performing some important task. McClelland found that an orientation toward achievement was usually associated with increases in achievement-related imagery in a particular test of fantasy that required subjects to tell stories about a series of pictures. Some of these stories, for example, contained extensive fantasies about students who were ambitious to become great surgeons, or to succeed in some other fashion, and they were more common in the experimentally created achievement atmosphere than in a nonachievement, noncompetitive one. Such findings suggested that fantasy behavior could reflect motives like achievement, at least under certain conditions, and could be used to measure it.

Now, it should be clear that fantasy is merely one type of behavior from which we might make inferences about a person's motivations. Subsequent research has shown, moreover, that the theoretical relationship between motive states and fantasy is complex, and that under certain conditions, the relationship, instead of being positive, is negative. In other words, sometimes people will inhibit the expression in fantasy of their motives (for example, when these motives involve social taboos), in which case some other kind of behavioral index is required to assess the motivation. But the effort to measure the content of fantasy and to determine whether it really reflects motive states illustrates the research process by which psychologists attempt to measure personality constructs by studying their behavioral consequences.

Thus far we have presented assessment as an essential part of personality theory-building and testing. Often, however, the aim of assessment is the prediction of behavior, especially when prediction is important from a practical standpoint. It may not matter at the moment whether the psychologist clearly understands the theoretical structures and processes related to the behavior he wishes to predict. He may only be interested in predicting as accurately as he can, and if he can do so without elaborate theorizing he may be satisfied for a time. We might call this aspect of assessment, in contrast with the measurement of constructs, *empirical prediction*.

ASSESSMENT AND EMPIRICAL PREDICTION

One of the most striking instances of successful research dealing with empirical prediction is the history of measures of intelligence. In the late 1800's in the United States, psychologists attempted to identify human activities that are the basic building blocks of intellectual capacity. They employed a number of simple sensorimotor activities, such as speed of reaction, on the assumption that the more intelligent the individual the faster his reaction time. Some years later, efforts were made to determine the correlation between the scores students made on these tests with their grades in college. There appeared, however, to be no empirical relationship, and the effort to study intelligence in this way was regarded as a failure.

At the same time, however, a number of European psychologists were using more complicated intellectual activities—such as comprehension, perceptual judgment, imagination, and memory—to identify the construct of intelligence. It became clear that a child's performance on these tests not only increased with age, but was also highly correlated with teachers' estimates of his brightness and with his school grades. It now seemed possible to develop a practical set of measures to predict success in school; thus, the Binet tests of intelligence, which were later revised to become the Stanford-Binet, came into being. The Stanford-Binet intelligence scale has for many decades been the most widely used measure of pre-adult intelligence.

The point about this history is that we are, to this day, theoretically quite unclear about what intelligence is. Intelligence is a hypothetical construct like other concepts of personality we have discussed. It has to do specifically with the cognitive capacities involved in adaptation. But even if the precise nature and origin of intelligence are unclear, we are still able to devise tests that predict school grades and adaptive functioning with reasonable accuracy, although other, nonintellectual factors, such as motivation and work habits, also contribute to learning, thinking, and problem-solving.

From the point of view of empirical prediction, we say that a test is valid when it yields a reasonably high correlation with the behavior we wish to predict. Thus, empirical validity means that scores on a test enable us to predict some given behavior. Assessment by empirical prediction then, is especially useful to us in applied contexts. It is employed, for example, when we wish to select someone for a certain job or for some training program. The field of industrial personnel selection is founded on attempts to predict success at various job levels, from unskilled laborers all the way up to executives. Whether or not we understand the basis of such prediction, we can readily test the validity of selection procedures by analyzing the tasks about which we wish to make forecasts and by determining the correlation between a given measure of some quality of personality or intellect and that task.

Often, of course, the theoretical problem of personality assessment fuses with the practical matter of empirical prediction, because we may base our attempts at empirical prediction on our theoretical speculations about psychological processes.

In sum, there are two reasons for using personality assessment devices: One is primarily oriented toward establishing and testing personality theory, and the other toward obtaining for practical purposes the highest possible correlation between a test and some behavior.

Before we pin down specific approaches, we want to make two additional general points about personality assessment. The first is that the technique we use and the way we use it are likely to depend, implicitly if not explicitly, on our concepts of the structure and organization of personality. Different theoretical systems tend to go about the task of assessment with different types of tools, and many attempt to measure different qualities.

For example, since a depth-oriented psychologist is intimately concerned with unconscious processes he is likely to choose a method that promises to be effective in getting at these phenomena. Hence, his preferred tool might be a so-called unstructured depth interview, which permits an individual to associate freely and to communicate inadvertently material that he might not readily express. On the other hand, a trait theorist, who is interested in consistent habits of response, might choose an objective questionnaire in order to get at characteristic behavior patterns. Finally, a psychologist who is phenomenologically oriented would give first place to introspections, perhaps those derived from a therapeutic context. It should be evident that the specific personality characteristics a psychologist seeks to assess depend on his theoretical system. Level of castration anxiety might be a very meaningful quality to assess from a Freudian point of view, but it would have little or no meaning in other theoretical systems that do not include the construct.

The other point is that personality assessors have traditionally inclined toward a trait orientation, even if unintentionally. The usual assumption in giving a person a test of any kind is that the quality being measured is characteristic of him, a disposition to act that he carries about with him—in short, a consistent attribute of his personality. This bias creeps in, in part, because assessment tests are always designed to reduce the influence of the situation on the subject's behavior. Our assessment tests, then, tend not to measure a person's transactions with his environment, that is, the interplay of situational demands and his adaptive responses to them. This implicit emphasis on traits may be one of the weakest features of traditional personality assessment, since behavior is a function not only of the stable attributes of personality but also of the external forces a person is exposed to. It would seem that ultimately the most sophisticated form of assessment must concern itself with both constant personality structures and the external social and physical conditions that interact with them.

Let us now examine some methods of personality assessment.

ASSESSMENT METHODS

Aside from observations in the natural life setting, we can gain information about the personality structure of an individual by means of three general methods: the case history, the interview, and the psychological test. Let us consider each general method separately.

The Case History

A case history consists of a story about a person that includes the main facts about his development, the important events of his life, and his reactions to them. These facts are then organized and analyzed along lines that depend on the historian's point of view about the organization of personality and its development.

It took one pair of psychologists 435 pages to record in some detail the activities of a seven-year-old boy during one day, and then incompletely. Imagine the multitude of things that would have to be recorded to describe what happens to a person over a lifetime. Description is complicated even further if we add the person's ongoing psychological experiences as he might report them. The point is that we must reduce the massive amount of possible information to those materials that are of prime significance to personality development. Moreover, we must organize this material in some systematic way, even while maintaining the threads of the story intact. To attend selectively to some things in a person's life history and ignore others requires a knowledge of, or concepts about, what is significant and what is not.

The assumption behind the case history is that present personality is the most recent stage in a continuous process of development. Therefore, the case history should provide us with clues about the experiences that have molded the personality. It should yield evidence of the person's life goals and the ways he has adjusted to the demands of living in the past as well as the present. The past, which in the case history is seen as functionally related to the present, can be tracked down through the reports of other people, through the reports of the individual himself, or through objective records such as school files and medical histories. The past can be considered either as the individual apprehended it (phenomenologically) or as it was in "reality." And if we compare the person's own impressions with reconstruction of the events from the reports of informants or objective records, we can often derive revealing information about his ego-defenses and idiosyncratic perceptions.

Most case histories include sections on family background (including siblings, parents, and grandparents), the attitudes of the parents toward the child and of the child toward the parents, early experiences and recollections, intellectual and educational history, symptoms of emotional disturbance throughout life, sexual patterns, positive and negative emotional experiences, aims and aspirations, occupational history, and, often, specific information that reflects the unique preoccupations of one or another theoretical system. This developmental orientation to personality assessment, retrospective though it is, is the unique feature of the case-history method.

The case history can never be entirely separated from another major source of information about personality, the interview. This is because the interview is an important means of developing the case history, in soliciting the information either from the person himself or from informants such as parents or relatives or friends. Thus, the interview approach is often basic to the case history and overlaps it. What does this method involve?

No approach to person-
ality assessment is more widespread or more versatile than the interview.
Because the skillful interviewer can roam over a wide variety of topics and
take note of the subject's reactions to those topics, it is a remarkably useful
method. Yet, the very versatility of the interview is also a source of difficulty
since no two interviewers are likely to work in exactly the same way. It
is therefore difficult to compare what two interviewers find out about one
person or even what information one of them obtains from different persons.
Since each interviewer approaches each person differently, it is hard to judge
whether the reactions of the latter are the result of the specific behaviors and
attitudes of the interviewer or whether they reflect stable qualities of personality. Moreover, since each interviewee will discuss different matters, it
is hard to compare them on the same psychological qualities. The absence of
standardized procedures in interviewing complicates the task of interpreting
the results of any one interview. As a result, efforts have often been made
to develop standardized interview techniques, especially for research purposes.

A chief difficulty of the interview lies in the reluctance of interviewees to
express their feelings and attitudes freely, especially when these involve
socially unacceptable impulses and behavior. But even if a person is willing
to confide in the interviewer, there are limitations to his own awareness of
important aspects of his behavior and subjective experience. If our theory
of ego-defense mechanisms is sound, then many of the most important things
we wish to know about a person may be inaccessible to him and therefore
unreportable.

An admirably clear and useful statement of the process of interviewing,
at least in a therapeutic situation designed to reduce resistances and defensive
maneuvers, has been provided by Carl Rogers. It is not necessary to adopt
Rogers' specific techniques rigidly or in detail to appreciate his astute analysis of conditions in an interview that decrease or increase defensiveness.
Rogers stresses that an atmosphere of acceptance and permissiveness fosters
the availability of the actual phenomenal field of the individual, and he points
out that in most social situations a person is afraid or unwilling to express
his true feelings to others. If he does, he is likely to find his listener evaluating
him and perhaps offering criticism or advice, so he clams up and expresses
only what he is sure will not lead to a negative attitude on the part of the
listener.

By being attentive the successful interviewer convinces his subject that he
is interested. He paraphrases and repeats what the interviewee says, thus
impressing on him that he is being understood. This practice, moreover, is
valuable because by hearing his own thoughts restated by the interviewer, the
person can become more aware of them. The interviewer focuses on the
feelings the person expresses, for they—after all—are the most fertile sources
of disturbance and psychopathology. Yet feelings are the most difficult
psychological materials to uncover, especially socially unacceptable ones a
person is ashamed of. So rather than *evaluate* what an individual says, an
interviewer *accepts* it so that the person will feel free to express more of

what is on his mind. Rogers points out that with an attitude of acceptance, the interviewer will learn more and will have more influence, and from a therapeutic point of view, the client will have a greater chance of discovering vital things about himself that he might otherwise not have known.

The general approach sketched above requires that the interview situation be to a very great extent directed by the interviewee rather than the interviewer, since the interviewer follows where the other wanders rather than purposefully guiding him and dominating the substance of the interview. Sometimes more significant information about personality is provided by this route than by a highly directive question-and-answer approach. As we have said, however, the disadvantage is that the unreliability of what is discussed is increased, thereby greatly complicating comparison with other interviews.

The interpretive problem of the interview is parallel with that of the case history in that we must choose, in sifting through the material brought up from an hour's probing, what is significant and what is not. The sorting here, too, is impossible to do systematically unless we start out with some notion, derived from a knowledge of personality development, of what is consequential and what is trivial in behavior and experience.

The interview is probably the most important basic tool in personality assessment and, used to its fullest advantage, it has qualities that set it apart from any other source of information. It provides an active, dynamic, two-person situation in which the interviewer is both participant and observer. It can also yield profound therapeutic consequences. These important and unique qualities are well recognized, for the interview is probably the most extensively used technique in assessment, and it is the most often used in validating other assessment tools as well. It has the tremendous advantage of enabling the interviewee to indulge in penetrating introspection while at the same time, because of its face-to-face nature, permitting the interviewer to observe his behavior as he introspects. For example, an individual may deny certain feelings but give evidence of them by speech disturbances such as stammering or blocking, by motor signs of tension and restlessness, or by physiological changes like flushing or paling . . . and the interviewer is right on the scene to detect these signs of emotion and conflict.

Efforts are being made to improve the techniques of the interview and to find better ways of systematically and objectively studying and analyzing its contents. Using film and tape-recordings to preserve the interchange between interviewer and subject is one means of investigating the interview intensively. Indeed, one of the most fascinating research problems is the study of the interview process itself. For not only can the content of the interview be studied but also its formal properties—such as interruptions, the time taken up by each party, and the expressive movements or gestures of the participants, which serve as a body language for attitudes, states of emotion, or moods.

The Psychological Test

The chief handicap of the interview is the lack of standardization of the procedures, and psychologists are continually seeking methods of solving this problem. Psychological tests evolved as a partial solution. In a sense, psychological tests are standardized interviews. They allow us to assess personality characteristics of different persons under comparable conditions. Although the content and procedure of interviews vary with the person being assessed and usually with the interviewer as well, a test is always given under fundamentally similar circumstances. The items or questions directed at different subjects are identical or equivalent. Norms show how large numbers of people respond so that comparisons can readily be made between a person being studied and others whose characteristics are known. The essential difference, therefore, between the interview and the psychological test lies in the standardization of content and procedure in order to increase the objectivity of measurement and to lessen variations in environmental effects on the results. While many professions, for example, social work and psychiatry as well as clinical psychology, have had a hand in the development of the case history and the interview, the psychological test is one of the distinctive contributions of professional psychology to the process of personality assessment.

There are a large number of theoretical and technical issues in the construction and utilization of psychological tests, though many of them are not unique to personality assessment. But these issues need not be detailed here. Suffice it to say that personality tests in particular are designed to obtain any type of information from which inferences about personality can be made depending on the interests of whoever is constructing or using the test. Tests of personality can provide introspective data, material for life histories, inferences about unconscious processes, as well as measures of adaptive behavior, physiological tendencies, capacities and skills, or achievements. Their chief justification lies in standardization and their disadvantages stem mainly from the limitations imposed by standardization.

A test merely forces a person to do something under specified, controlled, laboratory-type conditions and permits an observer to interpret the results in accordance with his understanding of psychological processes. Thus, the philosophy of tests is similar to the philosophy of laboratory experiments. The scientist wants to study psychological events *in vivo*, that is, as they naturally happen. The trouble is that he must often wait a long time for an event in question to take place, and it is difficult to identify, out of a complex naturalistic situation, the forces that determine the outcome. Many variables are operating in unknown ways to produce an observed effect. The advantages of the laboratory experiment spring from the opportunity it affords to make the event happen when the scientist is ready to record it and from the possibility of specifying or controlling the variables that determine the character of the event.

Similarly, by means of a psychological test, instead of going out into the naturalistic situation and observing the individuals he wishes to study, the personality psychologist can narrow his interest down to some specific aspect of behavior from which personality structures can be inferred. With the test he makes the behavior occur under conditions that he can specify reasonably well. These conditions consist of his own behavior toward the subject, the opportunities and limitations provided for the subject to perform on the test in question, the physical setting of the test situation, and the content of the test. Of course, not everything can be precisely controlled—for example, fluctuations in the subject's mood and situation when he comes to the laboratory to take the test, his expectations and interpretations of the situation, and sometimes even subtle, expressive communication on the part of the tester of which he is unaware. Still, appreciably more adequate control is possible with tests than with observation that takes place entirely in the naturalistic setting.

The fundamental assumption involved in the philosophy of testing is that the artificially constructed laboratory sample of the subject's behavior is truly representative of his natural behavior. The psychologist is not interested in studying the subject's reactions to a specific situation. He wishes to measure patterns of reaction or traits—that is, stable responses—under a wide variety of situations in real life. To the degree that this assumption is justified, assessment is useful and has general application. We can answer the question of generality in part by correlating test performance, or the inferences made from test performance, with what we predict or with what actually transpires.

An example of this generality can be found in some assessment research using the California Psychological Inventory, a questionnaire (cited in Chapter 5) that provides scores for a variety of traits of personality. The test was given to 300 male college students, divided into groups on the basis of evidence of the adequacy of their adjustment. One group was seeking counseling for personal problems, a second was seeking vocational and educational counseling, and the third group, presumably well adjusted, was not seeking help. On the asumption that the latter group was most well adjusted and the personal counseling group least, the three groups were compared. The adequacy of adjustment was indeed reflected in the test results, the well-adjusted group showing high or good scores in the appropriate subscales, the poorly adjusted group yielding low or poor scores. These findings are illustrated in Figure 10.

It is important to remember that personality assessment is of great significance because only through measuring the attributes of personality can we create and evaluate adequate scientific theories of personality. But it is also valuable for the practical prediction of behavior in many life settings. Predictions of great moment are often made about future behavior on the basis of assessment procedures. Personality assessment is, as is the entire science of personality, a recent discipline, yet recognition is growing of its importance as a systematic area within personality. This is only proper, for the success of the science of personality depends on the increase of sophistication in the technology of assessment.

Figure 10. CPI average profiles of male college students (a) seeking counseling for personal adjustment problems (------); (b) seeking counseling for vocational and/or educational problems (— — — —); and (c) not seeking counseling (————). (Data from Goodstein, L. D.; Crites, J. O.; Heilbrun, A. B.; and Rempel, P. P. The use of the California Psychological Inventory in a university counseling service. J. Counsel. Psychol., *1961, 8, 147–153.)*

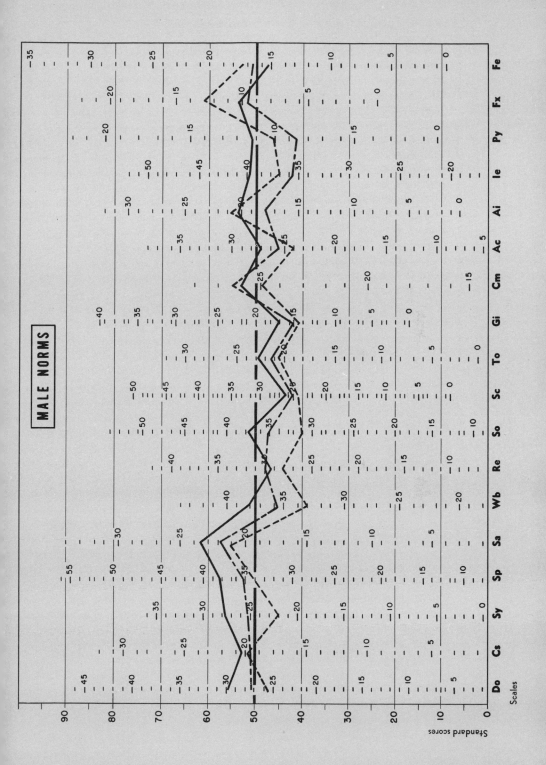

MALE NORMS

Applying Knowledge about Personality and Adjustment

One reason for the recent rapid development of the fields of personality and adjustment is the scope and urgency of the psychological problems to which the application of knowledge appears possible. This has been a mixed blessing, though, since it has often forced us to apply what we have learned prematurely. But as a self-conscious discipline the field is extremely young and our knowledge is still circumscribed. One of our most urgent continuing needs is systematic and creative research that will extend our horizons beyond the present primitive frontier. Yet the great bulk of our national resources tends to be funneled toward

8

those areas of science that involve the understanding and control of the physical world; relatively little trickles toward the social and psychological problems of living, including the very pressing modern problem of world peace and intergroup conflict. If our civilization is to survive and grow, however, our knowledge of personality development, the adjustive process, and interpersonal relations must keep pace with our knowledge of the physical world.

So, in addition to having natural human curiosity about people, those who do research in personality and adjustment often have practical motivations. If the scientist of personality knows enough about its structure and dynamics, he may be able to predict with reasonable success how given individuals will behave under given circumstances. And if he can predict successfully and reliably, then he can use his knowledge to control behavior. For example, if we knew precisely what produced mental illness, we might be able to control it by altering the causal conditions. Although there is no guarantee of success, since we are sometimes powerless to alter social or biological conditions, it is not unreasonable to say that control at least requires accurate knowledge and that knowledge often paves the way for control. Thus, as we are coming to realize, aside from the value of understanding for its own sake, understanding can give man tremendous power over the world in which he lives.

Having control over events involves an enormous responsibility, of course. Almost anyone would applaud the ability to eliminate certain evils, for example, mental illness. But if we could eliminate or reduce mental illness by altering the circumstances that produce it, is it not likely that we could develop other kinds of influence as well? We would have to decide what kind of personality and society we wish to create instead of the present one. It is easy, after all, to be against mental illness, but what are we for? The social and biological scientist, like the physical scientist, is beginning to discover that he must widen his perspective and concern himself with the social and personal values that are touched by his scientific interests and by his increasing ability to control.

Even the psychopharmacologist, who believes he might some day produce a pill to eliminate psychotic patterns of thought and behavior, must ultimately consider what kind of person is produced by pill-taking. The imaginative novel *Brave New World* by Aldous Huxley portrays the problem of what the world would be like with the use of "soma pills," the effects of which sound alarmingly like the boons promised in advertising by the modern tranquilizer. In any case, the ability of the personality psychologist to control human events even a little increases his responsibility to examine human values.

Of course, control depends on knowledge, knowledge that we do not as yet completely have. And if we truly believe in our own enterprise, we must believe that such knowledge, with the prediction and control implicit in it, is a genuine prospect. In fact, greater control seems presently possible, more possible than we are willing to admit, as demonstrated, for example, in the Chinese Communist's brain-washing efforts. It is interesting to speculate on this problem of control because it is altogether possible that we will some day have to face it.

Applying
Knowledge
about
Personality
and Adjustment

105

Let us bring this discussion of the implications of understanding, prediction, and control into more specific focus by considering some particular fields to which our knowledge of personality and adjustment is being applied currently and to which—most probably—this knowledge will be applied increasingly in the future. We shall consider briefly five areas: Personnel selection, group conflict, advertising and merchandising, public health and welfare, and mental hygiene and the clinical setting. In addition, we shall address ourselves to the question of applying psychological knowledge to our own personal lives, since personal needs often initiate our interest in the fields of personality and adjustment.

Personnel Selection

The idea of systematic personnel selection is at least as old as Plato, who, in *The Republic,* suggested that efforts be made to place the right man in the right job. As Plato realized, different men bring different qualities to their work and different occupations call for different abilities and dispositions. As soon as techniques were developed for identifying the functional qualities that distinguish people, the possible applications of personality assessment techniques were widely recognized. In personnel selection, the first step is to become familiar with job requirements in order to identify and measure the personal qualities that might be relevant to them. In a rough, often unsystematic (and unstandardized) way, the interview of a prospective employee by the employer represents an attempt to assess the applicant's suitability for the job.

One of the earliest modern attempts at sophisticated personnel selection occurred in the United States during World War I when the Woodworth Personal Data Sheet, the first personality questionnaire, was used on a large scale with potential Army inductees. The Army recognized that increased efficiency could be effected if it could screen out of military service men who were emotionally unfit or who were likely to break down under the stress of combat. Individual interviews were costly and unsatisfactory since too many trained people were required to do an adequate job. So the Woodworth questionnaire was developed (the questionnaire dealt with a wide variety of possible neurotic symptoms, and was the forerunner of modern, more sophisticated techniques).

Personality assessment procedures of this sort were used far more extensively in World War II, and they are still being used today for selecting officers, pilots, paratroopers, undercover agents, and a wide variety of other specialists. Industry, too, has used these procedures widely in recent years. The greater part of the effort in personnel selection has been at the semi-skilled and skilled levels, but this work is being extended more and more to the executive level.

The chief difficulty with personality assessment in personnel selection is validity, yet, besides that, the proper evaluation of procedures is an expensive and time-consuming affair. The field has burgeoned so rapidly that industries

Applying
Knowledge
about
Personality
and Adjustment

106

often buy selection techniques without having any opportunity to evaluate their adequacy. Nevertheless, research has often demonstrated that striking improvements in efficiency accrue to organizations that institute systematic personnel selection procedures based on personality assessment techniques. Since the general idea is viable, there seems every likelihood that the field of personnel selection will continue to develop, especially as techniques of personality assessment increase in adequacy.

Group Conflict

One problem that plagues organized society is the debilitating and destructive conflict among individuals and groups. Conflict is inevitable, though, when people or groups with opposing objectives interact, exist interdependently, or attempt to solve problems together. An example of this is the field of labor-management relations, where groups with incompatible objectives must work together toward their own and society's objectives; that they are often locked in bitter and costly struggle is not surprising. International tensions and war are a larger-scale version of this problem, and the antagonism between racial and ethnic groups within a society is still another.

Group conflict falls principally within the province of social psychology, a discipline that is concerned with the dynamics of interpersonal relations. Even so, since varying personalities are usually involved in these struggles, the problem also requires application of knowledge about personality. For example, we might ask, "What types of personalities are most likely to clash and what types will be task-oriented in the solution of their problems?" "Which individuals are most flexible and will most readily alter their attitudes and beliefs in interaction with opponents?" "What are the underlying, perhaps unconscious, forces that may be at work in a conflict between individuals or groups?" Systematic research into problems such as these has only recently been undertaken, and the psychology of personality has potentially a great deal to offer to their solution.

Advertising and Merchandising

A conceptual kingpin of most personality theories is motivation. Motivation is a matter of the goals and desires of persons, not only as stable characteristics of personalities, but as states that can be manipulated—that is, induced, intensified, or weakened. Seen this way, the psychology of motivation can easily be related to the fields of advertising and merchandising. For the advertiser is concerned with getting people to want to buy his product and the merchandiser hopes to devise the most attractive packaging of marketable objects so that people will buy them in vast quantities.

One bit of evidence of the burgeoning general interest in motivation research in advertising and merchandising is the recent best-seller, *The Hidden Persuaders,* by Vance Packard. Packard deals with a broad panorama of psychology in advertising, from advertising appeals about automobiles to attempts to get people to use products such as mouthwashes and deodorants by arousing their feelings of insecurity about social acceptance and capitalizing on their desire to avoid social failure.

Applying
Knowledge
about
Personality
and Adjustment

Public Health and Welfare

There is a far more lofty and serious aim to motivation research than advertising and merchandising, one designed to stimulate people to act in the interest of public health and welfare. For example, the United States Public Health Service attempts to educate people about various dangers to health and safety and urges them to engage in beneficial behavior, such as accepting newly developed vaccines or taking sanitary precautions against endemic or epidemic diseases. The agency must determine how to motivate people to accept public health procedures and abandon their fear or apathy about them.

For another example, it is widely broadcast that every day of the year and especially on certain holidays, large numbers of people are killed on the highways in automobile accidents. Massive efforts have been made to arouse the public about this problem in order to reduce such accidents. There is serious doubt that such campaigns are psychologically sound, or that they have the desired effect. It is known, for example, that fear-arousing communications typically drive people away from an issue rather than getting them to face it and behave more reasonably about it. In any event, here too, motivational research is oriented toward a very laudable and serious-minded goal. The point is that what we know about motivation, emotion, and personality has ready application in a wide variety of practical human situations where we want to manipulate motivational or emotional states.

Mental Hygiene and the Clinical Setting

An obvious place to apply the psychology of personality and adjustment is the field of mental health. Application here takes place in private professional offices or in clinics and hospitals with the intent to evaluate and ameliorate conditions of psychopathology. Many other public institutions, of course, are greatly concerned with mental health—for example, schools, prisons, and organizations that cater to the problems of the aged. Tied to this work of correcting emotional disturbances once they are created is the professional problem of prevention. Knowledge about personality and adjustment is pertinent and potentially valuable in educational and vocational guidance, in the problem of child-rearing, in the handling of the exceptional child (bright or dull), in delinquency, marriage and divorce, adoption, and the rehabilitation of the handicapped.

The great demand for answers to questions pertaining to adjustment has led to a tremendous growth in the supply of professional persons, especially in clinical psychology and in counseling. Clinical psychology as a discipline is covered in another volume; we allude to it here because its procedures are clearly outgrowths of knowledge in the fields of personality and adjustment. Indeed, clinical and counseling psychology are largely professional applications of personality research and theory to actual human problems.

Applying
Knowledge
about
Personality
and Adjustment

108

Each of us is likely to examine and evaluate the subject matter of personality and adjustment much more personally than, for example, the fields of engineering, physics, chemistry, or anthropology, all of which are somewhat more distant from everyday experience. There is widespread personal concern about mental health and the adequacy of interpersonal relations. People understandably hunger for guidelines to help them get along better in life. This hunger has led in recent decades to large numbers of books about personal adjustment. Some years ago, *How to Win Friends and Influence People* by Dale Carnegie and *The Mature Mind* by Harry and Bonaro Overstreet were best-sellers, and a succession of popular books by professional and lay persons has followed, including *Peace of Mind* by Rabbi Joshua Liebman, *Peace of Soul* by Archbishop Fulton J. Sheen, and a proliferation of newspaper columns and magazine articles advising people about how to be better adjusted or more effective in living. This outlook has often filtered into college textbooks that fail to present the psychology of personality as a scholarly discipline, but serve as inspirational treatises for the person who would like simple answers to his personal dilemmas.

Many readers who take up the present book may well feel considerable disappointment because they have anticipated a profound personal effect from reading on this topic. Yet they find in the end that, in spite of their increased sophistication about personality and adjustment, the same personal problems remain, the same anxieties, the same symptoms, perhaps the same uncertainties about the meaning of life. The disappointment occurs because simply by reading or by increased intellectual knowledge, we cannot produce major alterations in adjustment and relationships or develop satisfying life values. Indeed, it is doubtful that professional workers in mental health—psychiatrists, psychologists, social workers—are any healthier in their adjustment than laymen. Many professionals suffer neurotic disturbances or psychotic breakdowns, just as many lead happy and effective lives. Thus, simply knowing the principles of personality and adjustment does not insure that a person can apply these principles in his own life.

That is why books that promise to alter our lives by changing our modes of adjustment are misleading even if the advice offered has the ring of truth, is presented by undoubtedly wise individuals, and is psychologically sound. For example, it is certainly good advice to avoid envying or resenting persons who have more than we, and it is certain that a life built around such envy and resentment will be an unhappy one. Yet, no matter how hard a person tries, simply resolving not to envy or resent may have little effect, although it is often possible for him to fool himself about the truth of his feelings and impulses. Envy and resentment are commonly part of a deep-seated personality pattern that has a complex history and cannot be readily set aside.

Advice may be extremely useful in superficial matters where the behavior to be changed is not an integral part of the total personality. But it is apt to be wasted on the people who need it most. Of course, when a person's problems become acute enough, he can often obtain professional help. But the

Applying
Knowledge
about
Personality
and Adjustment

109

professional counselor has learned to be wary of offering advice since he knows that it can seldom be used and may even make matters worse. One of the most confusing and disturbing aspects of psychotherapy is that, when a client finishes telling his story and expects the therapist to take over the situation and straighten him out, no such thing happens. Instead, the client is enjoined to continue to examine his problems thoughtfully so that he can discover their nature and causes. He himself is expected to tote the main burden of responsibility for developing self-understanding and for changing his behavior from pathological modes of adjustment to more suitable ones. His professional advisor principally provides suitable conditions for self-discovery and change to take place.

It is worth considering for a moment why a person's intellectual awareness of general psychological principles has little effect in altering his personality, even though it may enlarge the scope of his scholarship and his understanding of others. One explanation resides in the concept of ego-defense mechanisms. According to the theory of defense, in adults, many impulses are in conflict with internalized social values and are therefore sources of great stress. This tension may lead an individual to defensive, stress-reducing efforts. These defense mechanisms, which are equivalent to self-deceptions, foster distortion or misinterpretation of situations and of the reasons for action. Often considered to be a characteristic only of neurotics, they are more and more being recognized as widely employed by even fairly healthy persons under conditions of psychological stress.

Let us consider an example of such self-deception and analyze how it prevents a person from profiting by good advice. Mrs. A, the mother of a young man about to be married, deeply resents another woman's becoming the major focus of her son's interest (a kind of reciprocal version of the Oedipus complex). As a consequence, she feels hostile toward the competitor. But such feelings and the impulses that generate them are apt to be in conflict with other values (for example, that she is a fair-minded mother interested only in the happiness and welfare of her son). Furthermore, she has probably long recognized, intellectually at least, that her son, if normal, is likely to get married, so she has known she would lose him inevitably to another woman.

When her son comes closer to a decision to marry, Mrs. A's impulse of hostility toward the girl will probably be heightened. As it is heightened, the conflict becomes intensified and perhaps even overpowering. She may attempt to deal with it in many ways. She may find other, more acceptable reasons for her resistance to her son's marriage, rationalizing that the girl is not good enough for him. If she resorts to the defense of reaction formation, she may not only deny that she feels negatively toward the girl, but she may bend over backwards to prove to her son, the girl, and most importantly to herself, that she has nothing but the most positive feelings. But her protestations of affection for the girl may well have a false ring, especially to the fiancée herself, who senses Mrs. A's hostility. The fiancée notices, for example, that when she comes to visit and feels she is not up to herself in appearance, her prospective mother-in-law and current rival is likely to go out of her way to point out how "lovely" she looks. On other occasions, however, when she knows she looks her best, no such compliment is forthcoming. Without knowing exactly why, she senses that Mrs. A is drawing attention to her defects even though on the surface she can identify only positive, pleasant, loving words. If she communicates her uneasiness to her fiancé, he is very likely to grow angry and disturbed and protest that she has no evidence that clearly vindicates her distrust of the older woman's sincerity. In this way increasing tension is created between the mother and her son's financée. The situation is one that produces intense unhappiness all around and may even wreck the prospective marriage.

Just imagine the naive attempt of a psychologist or other professional worker who has correctly sized up the situation to give advice to the mother. Even presenting Mrs. A with say, a gift copy of Sidney Howard's play *The Silver Cord*, which is a treatment of this kind of family struggle, would scarcely help, since it is unlikely that the mother would read into the story her own psychodynamics. In fact, she is quite likely never to perceive that the story in the play pictures part of her own situation. To do so, of course, would be to mount terrible distress in herself and to threaten the entire defensive structure she has erected for dealing with it. She remains insulated from insight because the problem is strong and deep-seated.

This illustration points up the main reason why a person's intellectual understanding of psychological principles fails to cut through to his own psychodynamics and why professional assistance for personal problems is so often recommended, rather than books that offer inspiration or wise analysis of ways of living. We typically resist insight as part of our protective cover over the sensitive areas in our personalities.

Not, however, that knowledge or even advice about adjustment is never of any value. But the utilization of knowledge or advice depends on whether the conflict or trend in personality it strikes at is weak or intense. A mother who is having difficulty disciplining her child can often be helped when someone suggests to her another technique that she had not thought of or did not know about. But if the advice carries implications that are alien to her conception of the relationship between herself and her child, her readiness to accept it is something else again. Similarly, a student may learn certain techniques of study or note-taking by reading books or pamphlets on study habits, but if the study problem is rooted in lack of academic motivation or deep-seated internal conflicts, such technical information or even exhortations to study hard are likely to be of little value. Unfortunately, most of the important problems of adjustment fall into the category of those that are relatively refractory to simple intellectual knowledge or advice.

This space has been given to personal applications of knowledge in the field of personality and adjustment because the desire to improve one's sense of well-being and effectiveness is widespread, if not universal, and untrained persons tend to misunderstand the uses and abuses of such knowledge. In this volume the author has not been presenting an inspirational treatment of personal mental hygiene. Rather, he has sought to produce in the reader a sophisticated awareness of the fundamental issues and concepts of the science of personality and adjustment.

It is fair to say that we are still in a primitive stage of knowledge in the fields of personality and adjustment. Yet the statement carries no adverse implications for the future development of the field or its rate of progress in its relatively short modern history. The possibilities remain enormous for the further growth of knowledge, and great challenges face both current and future generations of personality psychologists. We have been making good progress, for we are better able today to *formulate* the important issues than we were even ten years ago. Although the need for effective application is great, the need for clearer and better-supported principles that can be applied is even greater. Happily, these are rapidly being supplied.

Applying
Knowledge
about
Personality
and Adjustment

112

Selected Readings

Many excellent systematic treatments of adjustment and personality are available, and they usually approach the subject from differing points of view. Since these books generally attempt to cover the entire field, they are appropriate supplementary sources for most of the chapters of this volume. These are:

Baughman, E. E., and Welsh, G. S. *Personality: a behavioral science.* Englewood Cliffs, N. J.: Prentice-Hall, 1962.

Lazarus, R. S. *Adjustment and personality.* New York: McGraw-Hill, 1961.

Leeper, R. W., and Madison, P. *Toward understanding human personalities.* New York: Appleton-Century-Crofts, 1959.

McClelland, D. C. *Personality.* New York: Holt, Rinehart and Winston, 1951.

Shaffer, L. F., and Shoben, E. J. *The psychology of adjustment.* Boston: Houghton Mifflin, 1956.

Stagner, R. *Psychology of personality.* New York: McGraw-Hill, 1961.

In addition to these general sources, the following books and articles are suggested for each chapter.

Chapter 1
Lewin, K. *Resolving social conflicts.* New York: Harper, 1948.

White, R. W. *The abnormal personality.* New York: Ronald, 1956.

Chapter 2
Coleman, J. C. *Abnormal psychology and modern life.* New York: Scott, Foresman, 1950.

Gorlow, L., and Katkovsky, W. *Readings in the psychology of adjustment.* New York: McGraw-Hill, 1959.

Chapters 3 and 4

Allport, G. *Pattern and Growth in Personality.* New York: Holt, Rinehart and Winston, 1961.

Murphy, G. *Personality.* New York: Harper, 1947.

Hyman, R. *The nature of psychological inquiry.* Englewood Cliffs, N. J.: Prentice-Hall, 1963.

Chapter 5

Hall, C. S., and Lindzey, G. *Theories of personality.* New York: Wiley, 1957.

Munroe, Ruth L. *Schools of psychoanalytic thought.* New York: Holt, Rinehart and Winston, 1955.

Chapter 6

Anastasi, Anne, and Foley, J. P. *Differential psychology* (3rd ed.). New York: Macmillan, 1958.

Lambert, W. W., and Lambert, W. E. *Social psychology.* Englewood Cliffs, N. J.: Prentice-Hall, 1963.

Murray, E. J. *Motivation and emotion.* Englewood Cliffs, N. J.: Prentice-Hall, 1964.

Mussen, P. H. *Developmental psychology.* Englewood Cliffs, N. J.: Prentice-Hall, 1963.

Teitelbaum, P. *Physiological psychology.* Englewood Cliffs, N. J.: Prentice-Hall, 1964.

Chapter 7

Allen, R. M. *Personality assessment procedures.* New York: Harper, 1958.

Anastasi, Anne. *Psychological testing* (2nd ed.). New York: Macmillan, 1961.

Tyler, L. E. *Tests and measurements.* Englewood Cliffs, N. J.: Prentice-Hall, 1963.

Chapter 8

Fryer, D. H., and Henry, E. R. *Handbook of applied psychology* (2 vols.). New York: Holt, Rinehart and Winston, 1950.

Ghiselli, E. E., and Brown, C. W. *Personnel and industrial psychology* (2nd ed.). New York: McGraw-Hill, 1955.

Green, D. R. *Educational psychology.* Englewood Cliffs, N. J.: Prentice-Hall, 1964.

Lawshe, C. H. *Applied psychology.* Chicago: American Technical Society, 1954.

Rotter, J. B. *Clinical psychology.* Englewood Cliffs, N. J.: Prentice-Hall, 1964.

Index

C

California Personality Inventory, 54–57, 102
Carnegie, D., 109
Case history, 98
Catastrophic reaction, 44
Central motive state, 83–84
Character, studies of, 37–38
Character disorder, 25–26
Child-rearing practices:
    social classes, 89
    social influence, 90–92
Cognitive development, 74–75
Cognitive styles, 39
Competence, 18
Compulsions, 24
Concordance method, 79–80
Conflict:
    general, 5–6
    group, 107
    Lewin's classification, 8–9
    resolution of, 9–12
    sources, 6–8
    types, 6–9
Conflict and stress, 11–12
Conformity, 10–11, 15, 19, 20
Conscience (see Superego)
Consistency, 37–40
Conversion hysteria (see Hysteria)
Control, 47–49
Co-twin control method, 78–79
Crites, J. O., 102
Cue (see Stimulus)
Cultural relativism, 15–16

D

Darwin, C., 77
Davis, A., 64
Death instincts, 64, 67
Defense mechanism, 11–12, 20–24
    denial, 17
    example, 110–111
    learning of, 59–60
    table, 23
Demands, 4–6
Depression, 25
Development, 40–43 (see also Personality development)
Deviation in behavior, 15
Differentiation, 40–41
Directed action, 30
Discrimination, 59
Dollard, J., 58, 63
Drive, 58
Dugdale, R. L., 77

E

Ego, 48
Ego-defense (see Defense mechanism)
Emotion, 83–85

F

Empirical prediction, 95–97
Endocrine gland system, 85
Ericson, Martha C., 89
Erogenous zones, 64
Expressive movements, 30, 38–39
Extinction, 59
Extrovert, 56

F

Failures of adjustment (see Adjustment)
Family biography, 77–78
Fantasy, 65
Fantasy and motivation, 94–95
Fear, 84 (see also Anxiety)
Fixation, 76
Force-for-growth model, 66–68
Formal education, 89–90
Freud, S., 52, 57
Freudian theory:
    dream interpretation, 94
    "ego" in personality, 48
    personality theory, 41–42, 64–72, 90
    physical analogy, 33
    psychosexual development, 56, 76
Fromm, E., 68, 70

G

Galton, F., 77–78
Generalization (see Stimulus generalization)
Genetics and personality, 76–81
    family biography in, 77–78
    instinct as related to, 80–81
    studies of twins, 78–80
Goddard, H., 77–78
Goldstein, Kurt, 44
Goodstein, L. D., 102
Gough, H. G., 54–57
Group conflict, 107
Guthrie, E., 58

H

Hall, C. S., 62
Hartshorne, H., 37–38
Heilbrun, A. B., 102
Hemmendinger, L., 75
Hierarchy of needs, 67
Hippocrates, 52, 56
Horney, Karen, 7, 42, 71
Howard, S., 111
Huxley, A., 105
Hypochondria, 24
Hysteria, 17, 24

I

Identification with the aggressor, 90
Individuation, 68
Informal education, 89–90
Inhibition, 47–49
Instinct, 80–81